Wilderness

in the Lower Mainland

A Guide to

B. C. Forest Service Recreation Sites

by

Ed Rychkun

Rychkun Recreation Publications

ISBN 0-9681357-1-4

Canadian Cataloguing in Publication Data
Rychkun, Ed.
Wilderness Camping in the Lower Mainland: a guide to B.C. Forest Service Recreation Sites

ISBN 0-9681357-1-4

1. Camp sites, facilities, etc. - British Columbia - Lower Mainland Region.
2. Recreation areas,- British Columbia -Lower Mainland Region.
I. Title.
II. Title: A guide to B.C. Forest Service Recreation Sites.

GV198.L3R92 1996 796.54'0971137 C96-980423-7

Editing: Hope Rychkun
Cover and Photos: Ed Rychkun
Printed in Canada by Kromar Printing Ltd.
Front cover: B.C. Forest recreation site at Wood Lake

Published in Canada by
Rychkun Recreation Publications
23951 58A Place, Langley, B.C. V2Z 1A5
Phone (604) 532 5617

Disclaimer

This book is intended to provide basic information on British Columbia Forest Service (BCFS) recreation sites. It is designed to help you have safe and enjoyable recreational experiences. The book is sold with the understanding that it should be used as a general guide to help decide where to go, how to get there, and help identify key features and attractions.

The author has done extensive research to give complete and accurate information on each area, destination, and access conditions but the reader should be aware that these conditions may change dramatically from day-to-day, season-to-season and year-to-year. The maps and information provided should be used for general reference only and it should be understood that information may change with time.

Neither the author, Ed Rychkun, nor the publisher Rychkun Recreation Publications, nor BC Forest Service shall have any liability or responsibility to any person with respect to any loss or damage caused or alleged to be caused directly or indirectly by information contained in this guidebook.

Distributed by **Gordon Soules Book Publishers Ltd.** • 1354-B Marine Drive,
West Vancouver BC Canada V7T 1B5
•620-1916 Pike Place, Seattle WA 98101 US
E-mail: books@gordonsoules.com
Web site: http://www.gordonsoules.com
(604) 922 6588 Fax: (604) 688 5442

Contents

Acknowledgments

There were several people involved in helping me create this volume of information but once again my trusty navigator and exploration companion gets the credit for the most perseverance in finding some of these places, particularly those at the end of some of the tougher trails. These required some exceptional stamina to reach the destination.

But the most helpful, less conspicuous assistance came from the forestry people. Ruben Medeiros and Ken Langdale were exceptionally helpful and supportive, providing me with maps, information, and many details that would otherwise not be easily found. These two gentlemen must be truly commended, not only in their cooperative support of my plight, but in the efforts and dedication they exhibit in creating, and maintaining the recreational program in the Valley. When you create a book like this you come to realize that there are always some exceptional people working in the background, with little recognition, to provide the rest of us with unique places to see and enjoy.

Yet another acknowledgment needs to go to some special friends who supplied some of the excellent photographs from a few rather lofty elevations that me and my partner did not have the endurance to get to. Sterling Rychkun learned all about stamina when he tackled Flora Lake. Julian Houlding also learned the meaning of physical fitness when he and his friends tried the Pierce Lake trail, all the way to the top of Mount MacFarlane. They all contributed some excellent photographs.

INTRODUCTION

While stumbling around the valley writing my last book on lakes, my partner and I consistently encountered a completely different class of recreation sites that fascinated us. Most of these sites differed quite substantially from your typical provincial park in that they actually looked primitive in comparison... at first look that is. Several differences were obvious. First, they were always fairly small. Secondly, access was typically difficult. Most of the camping spots just looked like places that had been beaten out by random traffic. Third, information on these sites was also difficult to find. But there was one common thing we noticed - the choice of location. It was always special. And if you travel the backroads a lot you soon come to realize that special spots are not easy to find. Then we came upon a few sites that were absolutely staggering. Places like Twenty Mile Creek, Skwellepil Creek, Wood Lake - places most people never heard of - really made us stop and simply gaze at the beauty of the location. I started to realize that these places were not a mere result of random traffic. There was a purpose, and a consistency of design to these places. They were actually engineered to be this way! It was then that I began to appreciate the true nature of these sites and what they had to offer. It was then that I came to know the brown stake that marked a BC Forest Service recreation site.

These sites had yet another interesting aspect. They were definitely *not* well publicized even though there were 38 of them in the Lower Mainland. Information on them seemed as illusive as the sites themselves. As I found out later, these sites had been developed over several years under stringent budget restrictions. A little unknown section of the BC Forest Service dubbed the Recreation Division had been picking away, slowly building an impressive inventory of sites and trails. With little money for such things as publicity and development of provincial park-like grand facilities, the philosophy to keep things natural, small, and basic was a rather logical decision. That philosophy is very much the case today. The resulting sites developed under this program are super. Credit should be given to those who launched the program and continue to maintain it under low budgets. The sites create a unique class of recreational facilities for those needing to be a bit closer to nature than the average city dweller who heads for the big parks.

So now you know the reason for this book. I decided to share these places by providing the details on location and features. The area of interest is the Lower Mainland and the Chilliwack Forest District, which has 38 unique sites. This book will lead you to places especially selected by the Forestry. You will never find them posh but you will find them unique.

THE CHILLIWACK FOREST DISTRICT

It is worth while to provide a bit of background to the Chilliwack District and the forestry recreational program. The 1,168,000 hectares of the Chilliwack Forest District contains over half of BC's population. The vast area is bounded by Bowen Island to the west, Manning Park on the east, Boston Bar to the north and the US border to the south. The topography is dominated by the Fraser River and the western slopes of the Coastal and Cascade mountains. From a flat river valley to steep rugged mountains, the variation in terrain provides an extremely good area for recreational pursuits because it is abundant in streams, lakes, topographical variation and a diversity of vegetation. Typically the terrain rises from the flat bottom at sea level to elevations over 1500 meters to the north and elevations in excess of 2000 meters in the eastern part of the district. This, coupled with the west coast rain provides a most interesting forest environment which changes dramatically to sub-alpine around 900 meters and then alpine at elevations around 1500 meters. Carved out by the impressive rivers and streams, endless canyons and valleys are available to explore and enjoy.

Historically, this rough terrain has been hostile to recreation with little access available. Recently this has started to change. Much of this new philosophy on access has become possible because of the BC Forest Service. The Forest Service has traditionally been responsible for managing, protecting and conserving the province's forest resources. It has been committed to the integration of resources such as timber, range, water, fish and wildlife, and preserving them for future generations. Throughout BC there are multiple forest uses so the Forest Service focus changes depending on the needs of the district. In recent years the needs spotlight has been on the forest management, logging practices and conservation.

Through the logging management, and the control of development, the Service has allowed a network of logging roads to literally cover the Chilliwack Forest District. There are thousands of kilometers of roads reaching deep into areas of the District. This has been happening for almost 50 years. Many roads have grown in while many others are punched into the hills every day. Needless to say, these roads provide quite an excellent system of access and a new recreational interface to areas never accessible before.

THE FOREST SERVICE RECREATION PROGRAM

In 1971, the BC Forest Recreation Program was initiated to take responsibility for providing recreation in the crown forests of BC. Since then over 1000 recreation sites and thousands of kilometers of trails have been provided by the Forestry. This statistic in itself is surprising since it is little publicized. Perhaps the Forestry has remained a bit bashful about this but this is quite an impressive list. Most of the time the spotlight and publicity has been on the more glamorous Provincial and Regional parks, not on BCFS recreation sites. So the Forestry has gone unnoticed with regards to recreation.

Yet another aspect of the recreational program that has kept it low key, is the type of program. BCFS sites are classified as rustic. The Provincial Parks classification system classifies the facilities as "primitive".... a bit of a misnomer because for many these sites represent some of the most incredible natural places in the valley. The BCFS program focuses on keeping the sites small (less than 10 vehicle units). They are typically near lakes and rivers. They actually *design* their sites to blend in with the natural surroundings. When you see the camping pads, your first impression is that no one has really done anything here except to clear out some brush and place a biffy (toilet) and a garbage can nearby. Wrong. The access arrangement, the site layout, the access to water, and the choice of setting have not been a random process.

Although the sites do not offer sophisticated amenities such as you will find at most provincial parks, they are not meant to. The idea is to provide basic sanitary facilities, basic fire rings to contain fire hazards, cleared sites called "pads," picnic tables, garbage cans, and where appropriate, some form of boat launch. These launches are designed for a canoe or a cartop. Many places have firewood. The roads are gravel and in many cases very rough. In several cases, a 4X4 or truck is required to get to the site. By design, the access and facilities are basic, not engineered for a massive invasion of people. The result is that these sites present a rather unique opportunity to anyone who loves the wild aspect of the outdoors.

TRUE WILDERNESS RECREATION

The BCFS sites are situated in spectacular wilderness, offering true "wilderness recreation," typically requiring some extra effort beyond parking your Winnebego and walking over to the water tap. The extra effort is needed to get to these places. When you get there, the focus is nature not facilities so you also need to give up some of the normal recreational conveniences and rough it a bit. I place wilderness in quotes because these places are not truly isolated enough to be classified as wilderness but in comparison to other "formal" recreational places there is no doubt that many sites are as close to the definition as possible. The Chilliwack District has a team of recreational specialists whose challenge has been to protect the resource yet manage its recreational use. They balance the demands of the forest with the demands of the public, and in so doing have developed a wide spectrum of recreation values, opportunities and activities. Wilderness, scenic landscapes, and roughly developed facilities are the landmarks. The focus is usually lakes and waterways. Here the activities can range from passive enjoyment of scenery to the demanding challenge of mountaineering. Boating activities are kayaking, boating, canoeing. The roads are used for trail biking, hiking and 4X4 exploring. The sites encourage viewing, picnicking, camping, fishing, swimming, hiking, backpacking, motorcycling and hunting. In some places there are hang gliding and even windsurfing. Last but not least, the camera buff and the naturalist are always an integral component to recreation.

In this regard, the Chilliwack District, and their recreational group have done a commendable job in creating a variety of recreational sites that vary significantly. There are views that are unsurpassed. There are waterways for the passive floater and there are turbulent streams for the kayaker. The sites can be easy to access or require a 4X4. In the lower Fraser Valley, there are 38 of these recreation sites providing unique ways to interface with the wilderness.

DISTRIBUTION OF RECREATION SITES

The sites are most often carefully chosen, reaching into new areas opened by logging activity on crown land. The distribution of sites becomes more dense as it reaches the eastern end of the Lower Fraser Valley, with a particular concentration in the Harrison Lake area and the Chilliwack River Valley. Obviously there are fewer parks to compete with and the region has been less developed by the invasion of mainland population.

If you look more closely at the map you will get a better idea of the locations. Most of these can be driven to by a car but it is rare that you will escape some potholes and gravel roads. Only a few require a 4X4.

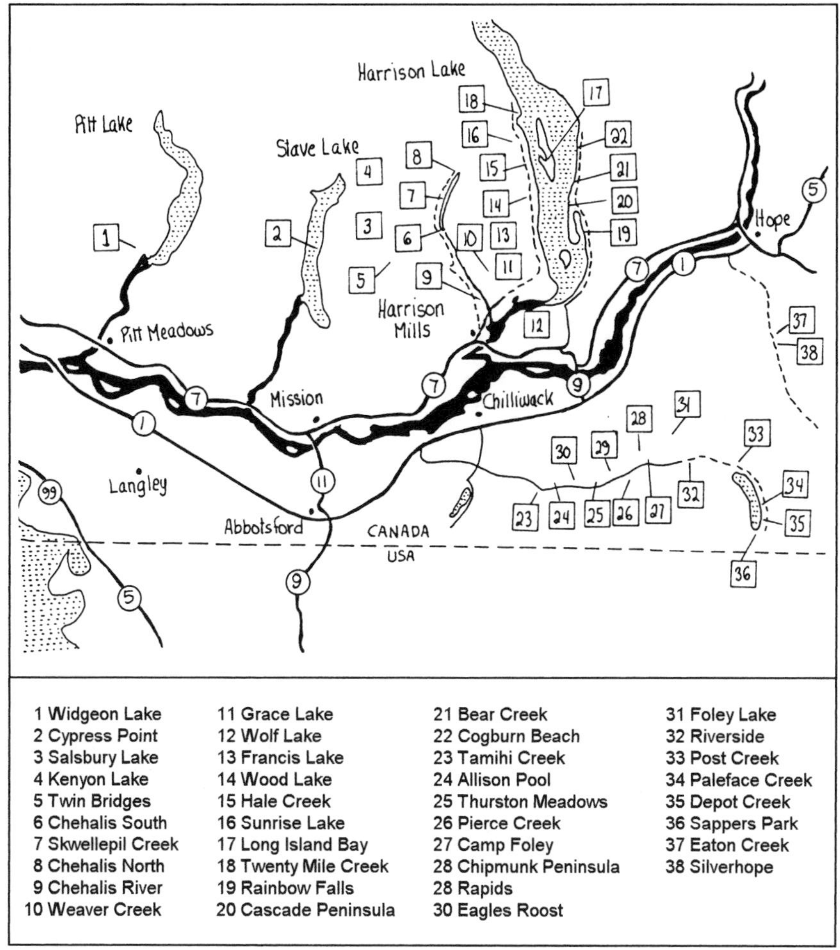

This book covers all of these sites. I have focused on only those in the Lower Fraser Valley, despite the fact that there are many more in other parts of BC.

USE OF RECREATION SITES

Now we come to the more serious information about BCFS sites. The Forest Service manages the forest for all of us. Many of the areas are being actively logged. And as already mentioned, the forest has opened up for our use through the management of recreation sites. But we, the typical demanding city dwellers, present a potential problem to forest preservation and safety. The simple tasks of driving on logging roads and staying overnight in the wilderness are much different than what we are used to. As a result, the Forest Service has de-

much different than what we are used to. As a result, the Forest Service has developed certain rules at their sites. Most of these are common sense but for those that may not be aware of forestry common sense, these are as follows. The act begins with the sentence ***"No person shall, when using any site or trail... "***

- discharge a firearm on or at the site.
- place or use any equipment on a site or trail in such a way as to impede or inhibit the use or enjoyment by another person.
- occupy or leave recreation equipment on a site or trail for more than 14 consecutive days unless he has written permission of a forest officer.
- continue, after being requested to stop by another person, to make any noise or permit an animal that he has brought to the site that is incompatible with the intended use and enjoyment of the site or trail by another person.
- continue making noise after being ordered to cease doing so by a forest officer.
- erect a sign or structure unless authorized by a forest service officer.
- deposit garbage other than that which he has accumulated during use in the garbage receptacle provided by the ministry of forests.
- deposit garbage on the site or trail.
- deposit fish or game offal, entrails, hides, bones, on a site or trail.
- take a dog onto the site or trail unless the dog is on a leash or otherwise under the control of the owner.
- do anything that endangers the safety of a person, damages property on, or is detrimental to the appearance of a site or trail.

This is not a particularly surprising list. The rules would seem reasonable but there are many who seem to prefer to purposely violate these, destroying the places and what conveniences there may be. In the past this has been a severe problem in that several sites had to be closed simply because they were being abused by a peculiar culture of 4X4 thugs and rowdies. It's a bit disconcerting to have your nice sedate setting fouled by some creeps who think they own the area and play music for the rest of the world. Flying beer bottles whistling through the fresh air can destroy the mood. In fact, this problem has discouraged the use of the sites by the real nature lover who really would appreciate the site. Instead many spots became secret gathering spots for weekend punks and drunks to dominate. Coming upon a nest of these is a bit of a chilling experience... it is much more relaxing to take your kids to the provincial park. Recently, however, the forestry launched an enforcement program aimed at policing the sites. These burly but polite forestry cowboys are very effective and helpful. Working with the RCMP if they need assistance, it is surprising how fast they can sort out a ruckus. The rules are enforced and the person who contravenes the rule is committing an offense. And believe it or not, Forestry Officers have powers to act.

SITE INFORMATION

BCFS sites are designed to be *rustic*. The improvements are kept to a minimum but always strategically placed... in a way that integrates with the surrounding natural environment. You may think that little has been done, but a lot of thought has been put into the place to leave it natural.

Sites are usually kept small on purpose. They are referred to as "pads," an open clearing where you can park or set up a tent. A majority of sites are selected for special natural attractions, usually close to a river or lake and are not large areas. Unlike provincial parks, the sites are not usually clearly demarcated but still identifiable in that the pad is cleared, usually accessible off trail or road and contains a metal fire pit or a fire ring of rocks. A *large* BCFS site will take more than 20 vehicles. These are actually quite rare. A *medium* sized site is designed to take 11 to 20 vehicles. A *small* site will accommodate up to 10 vehicles. Needless to say, because these sites are not large. Your best time for a peaceful visit is during the week.

Facilities will usually consist of one or two outhouses (biffys) and log-and-plank picnic tables. There may be litter barrels on the site. Some sites are posted as "user maintained." This translation is reasonably simple... pack out what you pack in.

Firewood is provided at most sites. You may bring your own or you may gather it near your site. You should get into the habit of *not* cutting trees... use only dead fallen trees and branches.

Boating is most often an attraction at the sites. Most sites have a cleared area or a formal gravel launch area that will allow you to plop in a cartop boat. This means that anything bigger than that which will fit on your vehicle, such as a canoe, small aluminum boat or kayak, may present a problem if you're not into weightlifting. In certain cases there may be a launch big enough to handle a small trailer. If you are attached to your cabin cruiser you will not appreciate a BCFS boat launch.

PROTECTION FROM FOREST FIRES

Every year human carelessness causes about half of all forest fires. An escaped campfire, a smoldering match or a cigarette butt can start a fire that destroys thousands of hectares of forest or risks life and property. The fact is that these fires are preventable. Hot dry summer weather increases the risks quite dramatically and the Forestry may even restrict travel, burning campfires and other activities in the forest. It is advisable to call the district office to get any information first, before you have a visit by an officer, or create a serious problem.

When you decide to make a fire, remember that you are undertaking a rather serious action. Fires should never be made without some thought. There are several simple rules that help minimize the potential problems for you and others.

- Do not smoke while walking; stop for a smoke break.
- Extinguish a cigarette completely on a rock or in the dirt. Feel the butt between your fingers to make sure no fire is left.
- Use your ashtray when driving on the roads.
- Respect fire closures and other restrictions.
- Build campfires only in fire rings. If one does not exist, make one... away from brush!
- Keep fires as small as possible.
- Never build a fire when the wind is strong.
- Tend your campfire at all times. You or someone in your party should always have the fire in sight.
- Always extinguish the fire before you leave the site. There is rarely a recreation site that is away from water so there is really no excuse for not using water to extinguish it.
- The fire should be at least 3 meters away from any log, stump, snag, tree or brush.
- The fire should be at least 15 meters away from any slash, inflammable debris or from a wooden structure.
- A pail with at least 8 liters of water or a shovel should be kept near the fire at all times.
- All inflammable materials should be removed down to the soil in a circle of at least a meter away from the fire.
- The fire ring, and fire should never be more than a meter in diameter, nor should the fire ever be more than a meter high.
- The fire must be completely extinguished before you leave, so that the ashes and any unburned material are no longer warm to the touch.

If you happen to see a forest fire you should contact the Chilliwack Forest district office. This and other numbers are listed in the back of the book.

BC FOREST SERVICE ROADS

The BCFS roads are an experience. They are much different than the public roads you are used to. Forest service roads are actually well marked, typically taking on the name and direction of the local area, river, creek or landmark. The Harrison West Forest Service Road is a bit of a long winded name but it certainly tells you where it is. Roads are usually marked with the brown forestry sign, and the sites are also marked. The roads themselves are extensive, primarily built for heavy logging traffic. The classification used by the forestry is based on the nature of the surface and the travel conditions.

These classifications are not too helpful because conditions can change quickly. The degree of maintenance, the weather, the time of year and the type of use will all change the condition of the roads. Some roads are not maintained at all. In many cases, the Forestry likes to place diagonal ditches across the roads to divert the torrents of water that like to carry all the small gravel off the road. These "loggers speed bumps" can be massive humps and dips after a while, forcing a need for good clearance on your vehicle.

Don't get too close to a logging truck!

Needless to say, early in the spring, the runoff will have cleaned much of the gravel off the road in places, exposing huge jagged boulders to test your clearance. By fall, the persistent 4X4 traffic has usually worn many of these areas smooth, or at least Goodyear rubber has! For this reason, my classification is relatively simple. I will simply tell you whether you need a car, truck, boat or 4X4 to get there. Another word of caution. Take a look at the picture on the previous page. As funny as it looks when you actually see the car, there is a bit of sardonic realism in its message. Many of the areas are actively logged and although these are normally open for public traffic, you need to be aware that these mechanical brutes take priority above all else on the road. And some of the drivers seem to take great pleasure in scaring little recreation vehicles. So pull off and keep away from these monsters... they have the right-of-way.

Most of the roads leading to the recreation sites are decent enough for car traffic and it is always tempting to take an excursion into the endless network of roads that riddle the mountains and valleys. These may be shown on the maps but they may not be maintained, blocked by washouts, fallen trees, even rock slides. One of the exciting aspects of BCFS sites is the exploration possibilities that open up to you with a 4X4 or a dirt bike but you need to take certain precautions when you try new roads because you will definitely not find any Shell stations or 7-Eleven stores along the way. Here are some tips:

- Check your vehicle, fuel and oil before you start.
- Make sure you have checked your outdoor supplies.
- Always carry a water container. If you are planning to gain elevation, make sure it is full.
- Take an emergency pack: shovel, hi-lift jack, tug strap, chain, air pump, tool box, jerry can with gas, rope, can of engine oil, can of gear oil, flat fixing kit. A come-along is nice if you have one.
- Make sure your spare tire is full and the jack is OK.
- If you are traveling into new territory, keep note of distance and turns. The network of roads is impressive. You can become disoriented and lost very quickly.
- Tell someone where you are going.
- Obey the road signs, you will learn to appreciate them since they are scarce anyway.
- Give logging and industrial traffic the right of way by moving to the nearest turn-off or pulling off onto the shoulder. If you happen to encounter a logging truck you won't have much choice!
- Drive with your lights on especially when the road is dusty.
- Watch for fallen rock, downed trees, blind corners and animals, including people, on the road.
- Stay with your vehicle if you encounter dangerous wildlife, especially those with young.
- Park well off the traveled portion of the road if you need to stop along the way.
- Always try to take a map.

- If you have a cellular, take it, it works on the mountain peaks.

WILD ANIMALS

When you spend time at BCFS sites you are usually in wilderness areas. It is safe to say that these areas are the normal home of many forms of wildlife, many of which you may even catch a glimpse of. There are several four legged ones that you need to pay attention to should you encounter them. These are the grizzly bear, the cougar, the black bear and the mountain goat.

In the Chilliwack Forest District, you will rarely see a grizzly bear since they inhabit the northern regions and more remote forests. Nevertheless some of the trails take you into some very remote, high wilderness areas so you should be aware of strays that may have inadvertently traveled south for the winter.

The cougar is more common than you would expect. Usually if a sighting has occurred, the wildlife people will post a sign in the area. A cougar will rarely attack and it will typically try to avoid people. They are most conscious of size.... a human appears to be just a bit too large to tangle with so their tendency is to avoid rather than stalk. If they decide otherwise, they will prefer small animals or small children. Always watch them and make sure that they are in the proximity of an adult. The Steelhead - Stave Lake area (Hoover Lake Trail) has had several sightings in the last few years but no mishaps have occurred.

The black bear is the most common in this area. Bears also avoid people but they will be attracted to food and garbage. With a good sense of smell, they can actually pick up the scent from a considerable distance. Normally not aggressive, the whole scene changes when a bear has young to protect, is feeding, or happens to be surprised. As a result, there are three main precautions when it comes to the fuzzy fellows.... don't attract them, don't surprise them and don't run from them. The last one is probably the toughest one to follow! Here are some tips.

Never attract bears There are several things you can do to make sure you don't set out to have trouble with bears. Their sense of smell is excellent and they can become very aggressive when camp food or grease is in the air:

- Never store food in tents. Leave it in the trunk, car or put it in a bag and hang it at least 3 meters above the ground and more than a meter away from a tree trunk.
- Never feed bears even if they seem friendly. They have no reason to be a Walt Disney actor so keep away from them.

- Sleep well away from the area where you cook food. They love the grease and cooked residue from campfires.
- Pitch tents away from dense bush, animal trails, lake shore and streams where they may wander.
- Don't cook strong smelling or greasy foods. Burn out tin cans after a meal by leaving them in the fire.
- Keep clothes and gear free from food odors and dispose of the dish water at least 100 meters away from the camp site.
- Always keep game meat out of reach.
- Keep the campsite clean by putting garbage in bear proof containers or pack it out. Burying it is a direct invitation to a bear... *never* do this!
- Always dispose of fish entrails by burning them in the hot fire or dumping them in a fast moving stream after puncturing the air bladder.
- Don't use or pack strong smelling products such as perfumes or deodorants. They can bring out the animal in more than one way.

Don't surprise bears I don't think most people will purposely set out to do this but you never know when this can happen. To minimize the possibility there are certain things that you should be aware of:

- Never hike alone or after dark.
- Never come between a bear and her cubs. This will definitely result in an attack.
- Never attempt to get a good picture, or good view of a bear just because it is casually minding its own business looking placid. It may not be for long if you surprise it.
- Be careful of berry patches, avalanche chutes and streams with spawning salmon. These are bear's favorite places.
- Keep your dog quiet, on a leash, under control. The dog can annoy a bear quite easily.
- Sing, talk, or make some sort of noise along a trail if you suspect anything. They will usually move away or you will prevent surprises.
- Be wary of hiking in high winds since the animals may not be able to pick up your scent... especially without your perfume and deodorant. You are apt to encounter them without warning.
- Leave any area where you notice fresh signs such as tracks, droppings or beds of dead animals.
- Leave any area quickly and quietly if you ever see a bear that has not spotted you.

Don't run from a bear This will be the toughest thing to do if the bear looks like he is going to take aggressive action. Here are a few tips if this is so:

- Never imitate a bear's posture or noises.
- Back up slowly and make gentle noises while waving your arms. More than anything try to stay calm.
- Return to your vehicle or climb a tree.
- Drop something such as your pack to distract the bear if it decides to charge. If this does happen, drop down, curl your knees up to your chest, bringing your head down and placing your hands behind your neck. This will protect your head. In this situation it is difficult to retain composure and you will have a natural tendency to run. Resist this unless you know you can get up a tree or into a protected place before the bear. Remember that running will trigger more aggression in the bear. Lying docile on the other hand gives you the best chance... believe it or not... this has been proven to be true.

Goats are also a rare find but not quite as scarce as grizzlies. They can be found in the alpine areas, high up above 1500 meters in some of the valleys accessed by a few of the trails. Mountain goats are not aggressive and they will normally shy away from any humans. The main problem is that since you are the threat not the animal. In a few cases, the goat populations have been disturbed by hikers. One such area is the Williamson Lake area near the Foley Lake recreation site where they have begun to leave because of human invasion. The suggestion here is to keep away and leave them alone. If you see them in the distance try to avoid them even though the urge to get closer may be there.

INFORMATION PRESENTED

This book is designed to give you the key information about the sites. In many cases the site is not so easy to find. I have therefore provided a detailed description in the section *"Finding the Site."* There is always a small inset map with mileage markers on it.

It is always of interest to find out what is at the site. In each case, in support of a detailed site layout map, I have described the facilities and layout. This tells you about the camping pads, biffys, parking, launch facilities and so on. This is detailed in a section called *"Site Description."*

Most of the sites have been chosen because of some special features and attractions in the area. I have attempted to describe these in a section "*Special Features and Attractions.*" Where there are nearby attractions and recreational offerings, these are included. In all cases a recreation site map is provided along with photographs of the area. The map shows the layout of the site, the camping pads and the location of facilities.

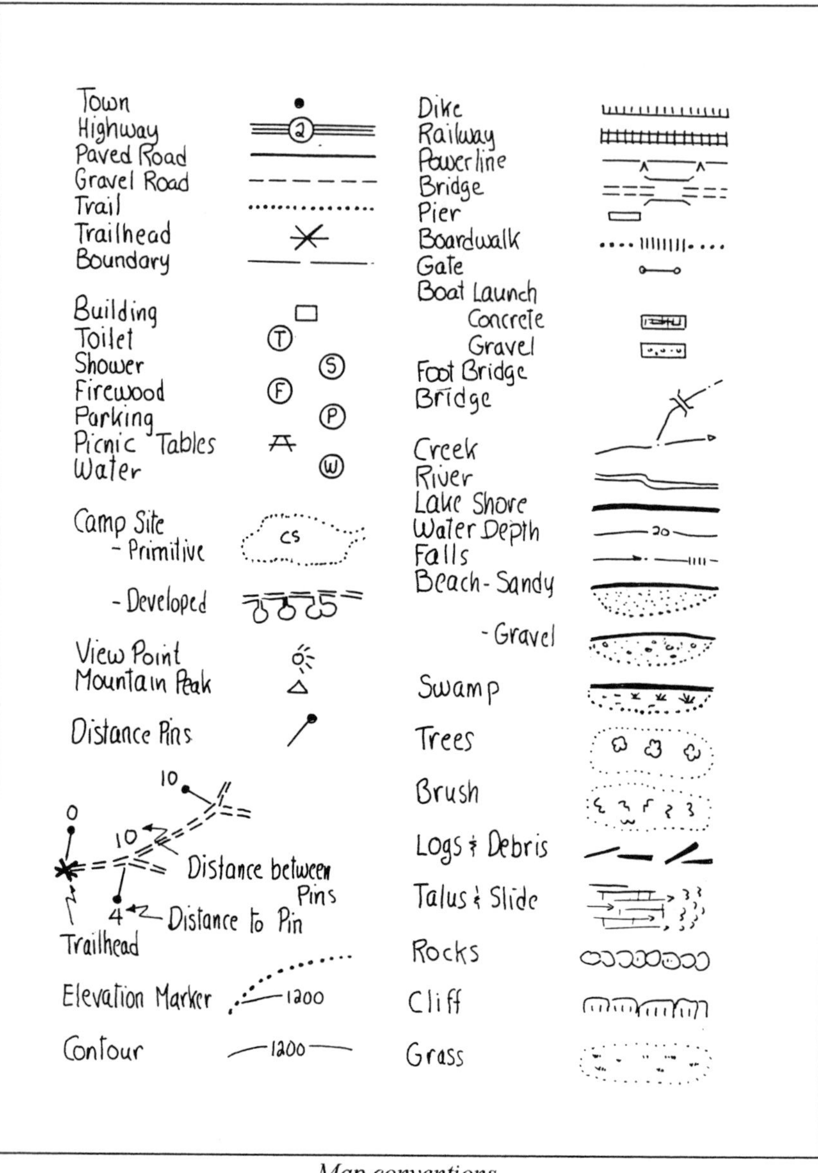

Map conventions

Oh, of course I try to paint a bit of picture of why this place is special… nothing that T.S. Elliott would admire, but it gives you a rough feel for the uniqueness of the area.

The maps follow a certain convention. First, North is *always* up. This is true north. Secondly, all maps are scaled with a scale bar. Regardless of whether you photo-reduce or expand the map, the bar will still depict true distances.

Third, the maps use a certain convention, or legend to depict certain features. Gates, contours, road, camp pads, trees, logs, etc. are drawn according to certain symbols and conventions. You will get used to these since most are common sense or you are already used to them. These are shown in the figure on Map conventions.

Hope you enjoy the sites.

Ed Rychkun

WIDGEON LAKE 1

☑ BEACH	☑ TENT CAMPING
☑ CANOEING	☑ SWIMMING
☑ BOAT LAUNCH	☑ VIEWING
☑ HIKING	☑ NATURE
	☑ SMALL SITE

The official site name of Widgeon Lake is actually a bit misleading since it is eight hiking kilometers away from the lake itself. Getting to the actual BCFS campsite requires a bit of a safari but once there you find that the site is a central hub for many activities. Picture yourself paddling your canoe through a tropical like marshland for an hour, skimming to a white sandy shore for a quick cool swim in clear waters. Then push your way upstream through shallower and shallower waters, heading deeper into the tall grasses finally arriving at the lone opening at the camping site at the head of Widgeon Slough.

The sometimes busy shore at the Widgeon BCFS site

Think about the dark night, sitting around the glowing campfire, listening to the chorus of nocturnal swamp creatures rustling about in the night. Yes, a real marshland safari, for a mere 4.5 kilometer canoe trip.

FINDING THE SITE The safari begins by first finding Grant Narrows Regional Park. The best access is via Highway 7 to Dewdney Trunk Road as you cross the Pitt River Bridge (first traffic light over the bridge heading east out of Port Coquitlam). If you are new to this area set your odometer to zero here. Turn left and follow Dewdney Trunk to the stop sign and turn left onto Harris Road (at 2.3 kilometers). Continue north along Harris (5.3 kilometers) and then turn right on McNeil. Follow this road through the rural area to intersect Neaves at 9.0 kilometers and turn left (Neaves is the same as 208th Street and it becomes Rannie north of McNeil). Now it is straight north on Rannie to its end on Pitt Lake. You will eventually take a curve right and encounter the huge parking lot at 17.5 kilometers. The boat launch area is at 17.7 kilometers. As you come up onto the dyke, you will see the south end of Pitt Lake and Grant Narrows. You can rent a canoe here in the summer.

Next, to get to the BCFS campsite at the head of Widgeon Slough, take your boat northwest to the little opening across the Pitt River (Grant Narrows) from the boat launch area. This is the only (and worst) section of open water where you may need to build up a sweat. There are two hazards here. The wind blowing down the river is sometimes a problem and the turbocharged power boats belting down the river are another. Both seek out poor canoeists in an attempt to swamp them. If you're not into canoeing it is possible to take a small motor boat up to the site but you will need to watch for shallow water in the slough as you head upstream.

After reaching the more protected inside channel behind the island, follow the eastern, or right shore into the Widgeon channel all the way to the next main split in the slough (at 2.6 kilometers). Follow the left branch and continue to the split (at 3.5 kilometers), then follow the right channel north for another kilometer. This will get you into the south section of the Widgeon Valley National Wildlife Reserve. As you approach the head of the slough, the water current will become more obvious. Typically, this will take you an hour unless you decide to dilly dally along the way by stopping for a swim.

SITE DESCRIPTION The main attraction is not the site but the Widgeon Valley and Widgeon Slough. Because the site acts as a central hub for the area, it is possible to visit Widgeon Lake and access several old roads or hiking trails into and above this spectacular valley. The site itself is not well endowed, consisting of an open flat grassy bench, offering a biffy, a few garbage cans, several fire rings and the gravel-mud beach adjoining the slough where you first beach. In total, the site will support about 10 camping parties in flat open grassy pads. Several trails radiate out from the site providing a wide variety of day hikes. From the beach, it is possible to paddle further up the creek to a large gravel bar.

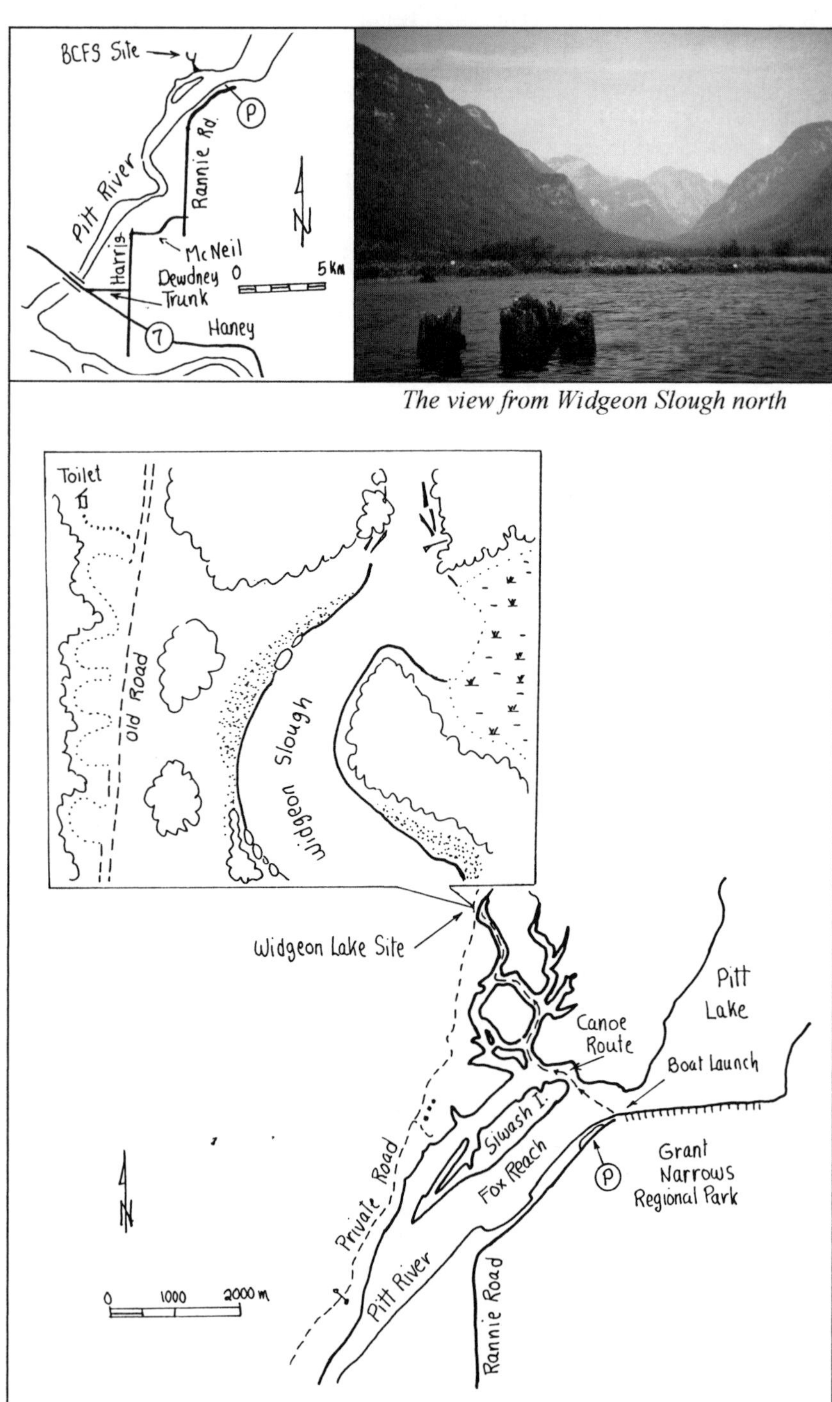

The view from Widgeon Slough north

This offers a quieter unofficial "overflow" camping area and there are a few choice spots along the left river bank on the way up.

SPECIAL FEATURES and ATTRACTIONS Several attractions bring many people here in summer. The combination of the unique canoe trip, the extensive marsh, the proximity to town, the camping, and the range of wilderness hikes makes this a particularly popular place in summer. It is possible to see this whole area covered with canoes. This makes it a bit unnerving to pitch a tent in such a flurry of activity. The poor recreation site is like grand central station. If you want to camp and really enjoy the place, pick off-season, then back-pack into the valley or head up to Widgeon Lake... even up toward DeBeck Valley and find a less popular spot.

Canoeing The trip is 4.5 kilometers, taking you upstream into the marshlands of the lower Widgeon Valley. The stream width varies from a narrow 25 meters to 130 meters in places, with clear, slow-flowing water typically not reaching more than a few meters in depth. Along the way there are several small patches of shore bald of marsh grass, covered with a fine white sand. These are typically small but clean and pleasant places, sloping gradually into the water... ideal for a cool swim. These can be found all the way up to the BCFS site and even beyond the site. You may find that space is at a premium along this stretch because the patches of sand are very inviting to campers who have decided to stay. When you take this excursion, plan to take your time on the way up (or down) to really appreciate this trek through the marsh.

Widgeon Valley National Wildlife Area Found in the northern reaches of the marsh opposite the recreation site, at the head of the slough, this vast protected area is formed by a split in Widgeon Creek as it pushes its water down into the floodplain of Pitt Lake. It is networked with small drainage channels that will appear and disappear with time. If you are adventuresome you may want to slip your canoe through these channels to observe the bird life... but be careful to remember your way out. There is *no* walking on dry land in this place. When you get to the BCFS site, the extensive marsh is directly across from it. Widgeon Creek continues another kilometer through a cool clear channel to a large gravel bar where it then becomes a real creek, disappearing into the thickets. This section skirting the marsh is an interesting ecological area to paddle through and browse for bird life.

Hiking trails There are several excellent hiking trails including an old road system accessible directly from the recreation site. The *Widgeon Bowl Trail*, the *Widgeon Lake Trail*, the *Widgeon Valley Road*, and the *Widgeon Falls Trail.*

The *Widgeon Falls Trail* is the official BCFS trail. It departs from the old logging road to head east towards Widgeon Creek, then turns north to parallel the creek's upper west bank. The creek has carved a wide gorge through the valley big enough to allow the water channel to meander, particularly in summer. As a result there are several places dominated by extensive gravel bars interspersed with pools. From the trail it is possible to take a few diversions down to the creek bed for a dip. In the summer most of the channel is dry but during the rainy season the creek can become a raging torrent. The trail starts at 40 meters in elevation and slowly ascends to 80 meters following the grade of the creek. The vegetation is thick and lush all the way to the end where you will find the upper and lower falls, the feature attraction. Here you can take a cool dip and try for a fish, depending on the season and the regulations. Total length is 2.7 kilometers. If you walk at a good pace, it will take a mere 45 minutes one way. As a side note, there are several connections with the old logging road, providing an alternative return route back to the trailhead.

The *Widgeon Bowl Lookout Trail* is a relative newcomer in the area. It climbs mercilessly up to a viewpoint halfway up the Burke Ridge. The trailhead can be found behind the camping area, right across from the canoe landing at the forestry site. Designed for Olympic athletes and mountain goats, the footpath will lift you up to about 700 meters in a short 2 kilometers. You will alternate between gasps for air from the climb and the spectacular views of the Pitt Lake.

The *Widgeon Valley logging road* is one of several old logging roads in the area, the main one following Widgeon Creek over 10 kilometers deep into the DeBeck Valley to the north. Heading north of the campsite you hike along an easy flat slope through thick forest for the first 4 kilometers. Lifting you from about 40 meters to 150 meters in elevation, the road takes you past the lower falls where you will encounter a trail branch left to Widgeon Lake. But continuing on the old road, it is possible to hike at least another 6 kilometers up the main branch of the Widgeon Creek deep into the valley, with little extra elevation gain. This will take you past an area where you will find snow caves. From the end of this trail a new extension is planned to reach into the next valley at DeBeck Creek.

The *Widgeon Lake Trail* to the lake can be found just before you cross the bridge at Widgeon Creek (about 4 kilometers north of the campsite). From here it is another 4 kilometers to the lake. The trail takes off from the old road at around 110 meters in elevation, then rises to around 200 meters about half way to the lake. As your quads scream to make the final assault to an elevation of 770 meters you will finally cross the creek and curl around to emerge at the south end of the lake. The grand finale' is the last section which tests how well your quads have warmed up. You need to be in good shape since you will have to climb up the final rock wall before the lip of the lake. The trail is 8 kilometers one way and will take you about 4 hours from the BCFS site.

Widgeon Lake At 773 hectares, this lake is a large body of water, very deep and incredibly beautiful. The crystal clear waters plunge to depths of 120 meters in the middle, guarded by equally steep shorelines that thrust upwards to 1200 and 1400 meters in elevation along the north and west ridges. Add to this a lush cloak of forest dotted with craggy cliffs and you have a most spectacular place to camp, like nowhere else on earth. Facilities at the lake are natural. That is, with the exception of the open areas left by overnight visitors, there are no formal organized facilities developed here. There are several open pads worn nude of underbrush by many prior campers, probably better placed, more picturesque and functional than any developed park facilities. Fresh water is available and you have tree cover so what else do you need? After all, this is remote wilderness, a magic place where you can really get away and become one with nature. Probably the most impressive section is the upper falls where the creek forms a pond, then plunges down the rocks into the valley.

CYPRESS POINT 2

- ☑ CANOEING
- ☑ FISHING
- ☑ BOATING
- ☑ TENT CAMPING
- ☑ RECREATION VEHICLES
- ☑ TRAIL BIKING

Cypress Point is a most peculiar place found on the remote eastern shores of Stave Lake. It is the only public access point to this massive lake on the east side. Vividly illustrating a struggle between man and nature, this place presents a bizarre combination of pristine rugged wilderness and strange victims caused by the original flooding to create the lake. The result, in many parts of the massive waterway, is to present an unusual visual spectacle of strange unsightly landscape features such as deadheads and ghostly stumps or accumulated debris contrasted against clear blue waters and shear rock bluffs that drop sharply into the depths of the lake. Cypress is a special spot that projects out into the lake, formed by the fury of Salsbury Creek. The resulting gravel bar struggles against the lake to slowly hide the unsightly graveyard of trees. Oddly enough this place has a magic appeal to it... a fantastic place to get away from it all.

Approaching Cypress Point, a ghostly mix of nature

FINDING the SITE To get to the site you will require a truck. Make sure you are adequately gassed-up—the total return trip is 70 kilometers from the highway. In many places the prolific alders have made the road narrow and there are a few rough spots requiring good vehicle clearance. Off Highway 7 in Hatzic, take a left on Sylvester Road, zero out the odometer, and drive to the end of Sylvester Road into the Davis Lake Provincial Park. This changes to the Lost Creek forest service road. You will pass the Davis Lake access road at 18.5 kilometers. Continue on the main road. Two more spur roads are there to confuse you, one at 21.6 kilometers where you keep right and one at 22.3 kilometers where you should keep left. After crossing Lost Creek at 24 kilometers, you will pass the left fork to Twin Lakes. Keep right until you reach the main branch at 25.0 kilometers. The forest service signpost should be evident here.

To reach Cypress Point take the left branch and follow it, ignoring any small spur roads. At 27.5 kilometers keep left (right takes you to the west BCFS site on Salsbury Lake). Continue to follow this narrow road to 33.5 kilometers. As you travel this section you may wonder if you are on the right road but keep your faith and you will begin to see glimpses of Stave Lake in the distance. The road slopes gradually for most of its distance. At 33.5 kilometers you will be directly above the spectacular lakeshore. Take a sharp right turn and the Cypress Point spectacle will slowly come into view at 34.3 kilometers.

SITE DESCRIPTION The main site is on lakeshore, a large open gravel parking lot that doubles as a picnic site and open camping pads. It is possible to park a recreation vehicle here. This is a flat bench overlooking a large gravel bar formed by Salsbury Creek that has carved its way through the huge boulders and rocks, pushing vast amounts of material into the lake. As a result, the creek has pushed a long gravel bar out into the lake allowing one to reach the deeper water. Just below the parking area a pathway curls down and around into the heavily treed area at lake elevation. This is a small area but it presents a fantastic natural forest setting for a scarce number of campsites. Salsbury Creek is to the right of the camp pads and the large gravel jetty is straight ahead. The site has a few picnic tables, garbage bins and the familiar green biffy. I believe there is a short trail from the Salsbury bridge to the rock cliff across from the gravel bar.

SPECIAL FEATURES and ATTRACTIONS The main attraction is Stave Lake itself which is not easily accessible on this side. On this side of the lake this is the only public spot accessible by vehicle, even though Stave Lake is the largest in this area covering a vast expanse of 4410 hectares. Managed by BC Hydro, the lake was created as part of the Stave Falls hydroelectric

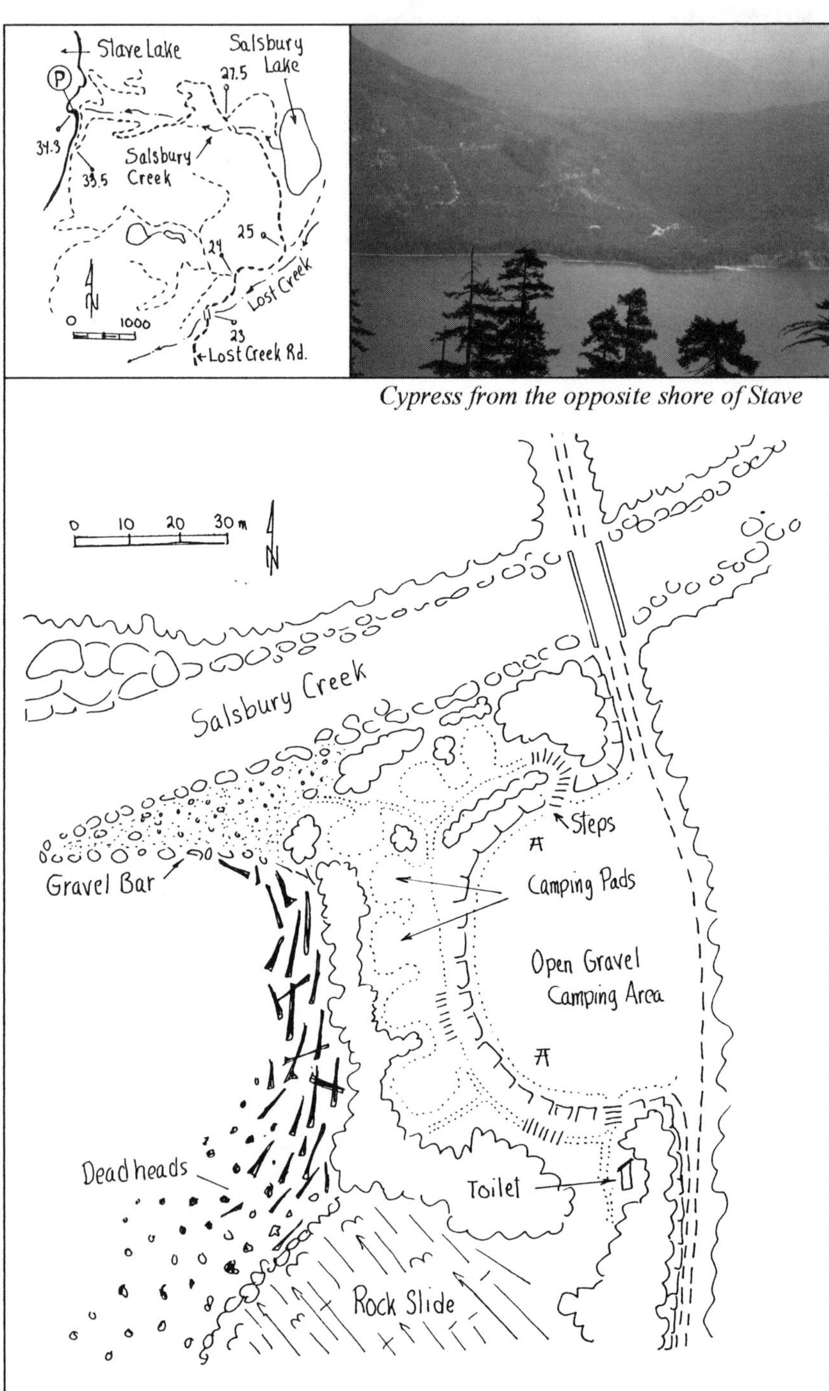

Cypress from the opposite shore of Stave

project undertaken between 1908 and 1921. The lake is long, 27 kilometers, reaching deep into inaccessible wilderness. The lake's main body is essentially isolated and mostly inaccessible except by large boats. Since the lake is man-made, the flooding process inundated vast stands of timber. At that time, it was not mandatory to clear the land prior to flooding so there are many areas where ghostly gnarled remains of dead trees and roots poke up through the surface waters. In other places you will find sheer rock cliffs several hundred meters high plunging the same distance deep into the lake.

Boating The gravel bar forms a natural projection into the cool, clear waters of the lake, with the crystal-clear waters of Salsbury Creek flowing along the boulders and sand. On the other side you see the ghostly forms of trees and dead stumps in the bay. This natural structure will allow you to launch a canoe or small vessel easily. Access from the parking area involves a short, steep trail which makes larger boat launching difficult. A canoe is more appropriate, so forget about using a trailer or a larger boat. Just in this immediate area you find an incredible variation in shoreline to explore.

A word of caution, however. The deadheads and winds are your worst enemies here. Remember that the lake is vast, in the remote wilderness, very deep, with **no** civilization along shorelines. The winds can get fierce as they blow down from the northern glaciers and there are many areas where the lake is filled with vast expanses of hidden deadheads that resulted from the original flooding—the little bay at Cypress is a good example of the ghostly boat obstacles—so the lake can be as hostile as it is beautiful. There are many tragic stories of people meeting foul winds and weather. Ironically, the best bet is to hug the shore and keep a sharp eye on subsurface.

Fishing As to fishing, the lake contains all types including Rainbow, Dolly, Cutthroat and Steelhead. Apparently the cutthroat can range to 50 centimeters and the dollys are massive. The lake is so huge that it contains just about every type of fish that can live in the valley. There is actually no reason for the fisheries to stock the lake since it is a natural habitat, but they obviously decided to add some Steelhead. To fish this lake from Cypress your best strategy is close to shore and head for creek outlets since you will not have a large boat.

Trail biking This area is virtually riddled with old logging roads, many of which are still maintained, but most have been abandoned. The views, the numerous roaring streams and the variety of valleys in this area create some of the best backroads terrain available in the valley. The road continues forwards up the mountain from the site and backwards up over the ridge to Twin Lakes and the Lost Creek forest service road from where you came. They are in rough shape. There are many washouts, fallen rocks and logs to offer you and your bike a chance for lift off... so caution is your best companion.

SALSBURY LAKE 3

- ☑ CANOEING
- ☑ FISHING
- ☑ BOAT LAUNCH
- ☑ BOATING
- ☑ TENT CAMPING
- ☑ RECREATION VEHICLES
- ☑ TRAIL BIKING
- ☑ SMALL SITE

Set in the vast Douglas Forest east of Stave Lake, in a large open valley, Salsbury Lake has not been a particularly popular place, obviously escaping the public for many years... even though it is reasonably accessible. Perhaps it is the fact that this fairly large lake is in an actively logged area contrasting its clear blue waters against the scarred clear-cut mountains. But despite this, the lake is beautiful. It is large and it is shallow, lined with thick vegetation... a perfect environment for fish. The depth is just perfect for lush aquatic vegetation to flourish, at exactly the right depth for trout. This paints a canoeing and fishing haven for those who visit the two small recreation sites carved into opposite shores.

The smooth waters of Salsbury on a quiet day

FINDING the SITE Take your truck (although a car will make it in summer) along the main Lost Lake service road from the end of Sylvester Road, off

Highway 7 past Hatzic (east of Mission). The pavement gives way to Lost Creek forest service road and you will click by Davis Lake at 18.5 kilometers. At 21.6 kilometers you keep right and, at 22.3 kilometers, you keep left. After crossing Lost Creek, you will encounter a fork at 24 kilometers (left fork goes to Twin Lakes). Keep right until you reach the main split at 25.0 kilometers. The brown forest service signpost should be evident here. Now, decide between the *west* BCFS site or the *east* site.

The *east* site has the easiest and best access. It is on the right branch where, at 26.5 kilometers, you will reach a good-sized gravel parking lot and the BCFS campsite. If you are driving a good sized recreation vehicle this is the perfect place for you since the large gravel pad is beside the main road and it is a mere 75 meters away from the lake where a good gravel trail has been punched through the third growth.

To get to the *west site*, take the left branch (back at the 25-kilometer mark) to 27.6 kilometers and turn right toward the lake. Keep right to curve back at 28 kilometers and continue straight through to finally turn left at 28.7 kilometers. You will really wonder if there is anything here because the lake is not visible but the BCFS site is just a short distance in, with a small (three- to four-truck) parking lot overlooking the lakeshore.

SITE DESCRIPTION There are two small, semi-open sites on the east and west shores. The main site is on the east road where there is a good-sized gravel parking lot adjacent to the main road with a toilet and garbage can. The gravel pullout is large enough for large campers. From here the gravel walkway is just across the road so you can carry a cartop boat 75 meters to the lakeshore. At lakeshore there is a small gravel beach (and I mean small!) that serves as both camp pad and place to launch a small boat. There are a few open pads scattered in the trees to the right, good enough to service three or four parties. I am not really sure whether these are official BCFS pads or just beaten turf but the sites are positioned nicely in natural settings right at the shore. A small stream borders the campsite area, providing fresh water. The shore is usually lined with debris so you may have to haul your boat over the top of the logs *and* the party that beat you to the prime spot.

The west side is a bit different, with a small parking lot right at lakeshore, large enough to park about four vehicles at most. This also serves as a camp pad so the first one there could dominate the whole pad making it difficult for neighbors. There are a few gravel campsites/parking areas back away from the main pad but you will be surrounded by hostile brush and thickets. On this side the brush is thick, hiding the old fallen and cut logs. You will therefore not find it easy to seek out any other spots in the bush. The site has a biffy and a garbage can.

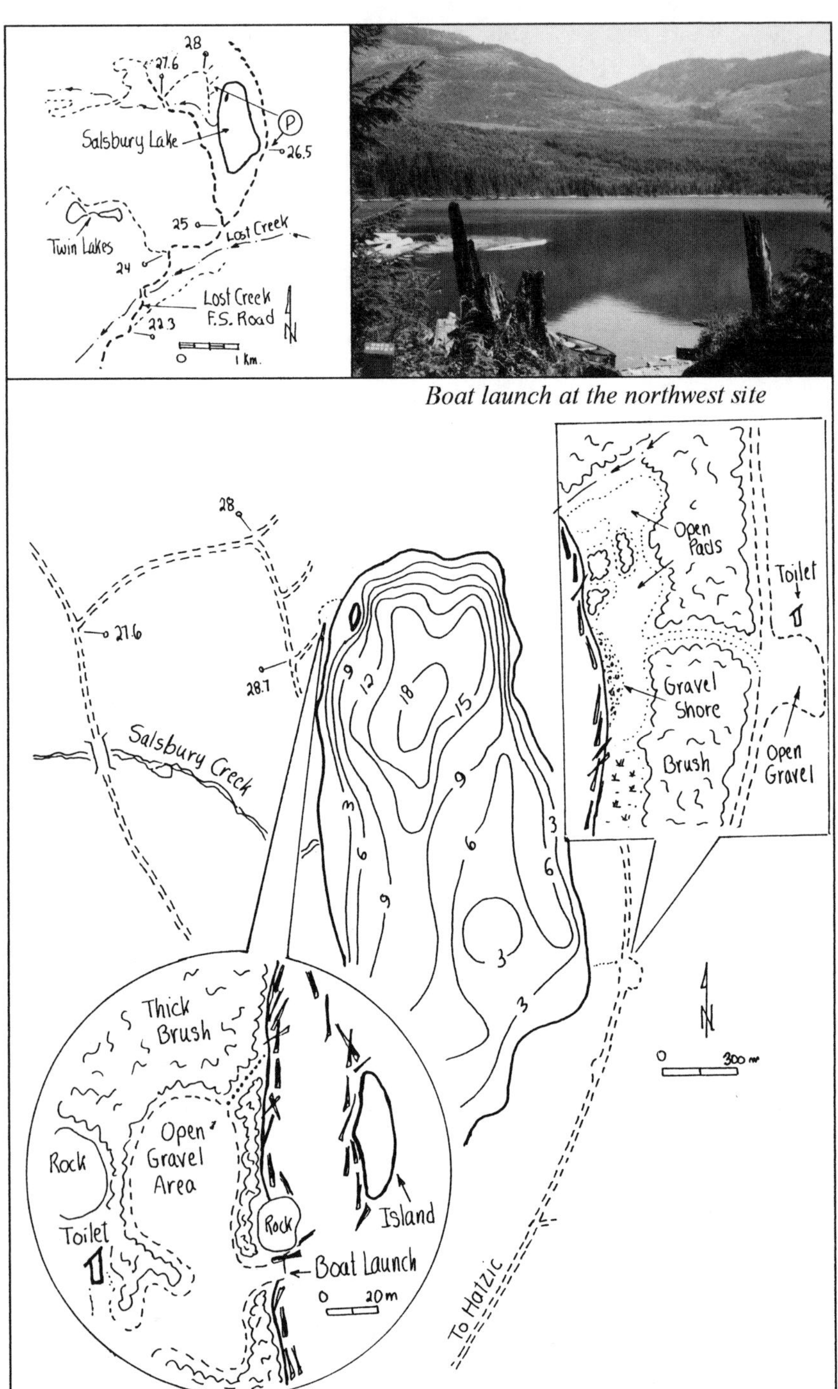

Boat launch at the northwest site

There is also a short gravel drop to the lakeshore that serves as a launch. It is possible to back a small trailer into this spot but blown in logs may inhibit your entry directly into the very shallow water. The other inhibitor is how cooperative the other inhabitants are with their parked vehicle that may block turning around. A cartop boat or canoe can be slipped in easily at this point.

SPECIAL FEATURES and ATTRACTIONS Salsbury Lake is a large lake measuring 79 hectares and situated at an elevation of 409 meters, reasonably high up. This lake sits in an intensely logged plateau, located in a large, flat, open basin southwest of towering Mount Jasper, leaving the lake exposed to strong winds. Although the shoreline is somewhat protected by the trees, they obviously have not been able to stop the winds that have spent much of their energy blowing logs and debris around the lake lining almost all of the shoreline. Despite its size, this lake is quite shallow, averaging only 7.5 meters and reaching a maximum depth of 19 meters at the north end. This makes the whole lake and its long rough shoreline a fantastic place to explore with a small boat.

Boating Two places at the BCFS sites allow you to launch a cartop or canoe. Due to the size of the lake and its shallowness it offers a paradise of aquatic life and beauty to paddle through and explore. Once you get onto the lake, you can easily lose yourself in the natural quiet. The shallowness of the lake is something to always be aware of. It is not a good place to try out the big Mercruiser—you may find a foreign object poking through your hull.

Fishing An aggressive program was started in 1988 in an attempt to bring life to this once-barren lake. An added bonus is the number of kokanee that have been placed in the lake, obviously a special experiment. The shoreline is not easy to fish from since logs and brush are a dominant problem. You are pretty well dependent on a boat or float device. Almost all the lake is shallow except for the north end which reaches 19 meters just beyond the big rock opposite the boat launch. For this reason, the better shore fishing will be at this big rock where it is possible to cast... if you can get to the rock island.

Trail biking This area is a vast network of logging roads, many still maintained, but most abandoned. There are few places not reached by roads, offering a variety of peaks and valleys to explore on a bike. The views, the mountain streams and the variety of rugged terrain in the immediate area makes this another one of the best biking alternatives in the valley. It is another biker and four-wheeler paradise so if you are coming up here to camp or fish, be sure to bring your bikes.

KENYON LAKE 4

- ☑ CANOEING
- ☑ FISHING
- ☑ BOAT LAUNCH
- ☑ TENT CAMPING
- ☑ TRAIL BIKING
- ☑ SMALL SITE

Finding this lake is just as dramatic an experience as first seeing it. Anyone who loves fly fishing may have a minor stroke when they see this fisherman's dream lake appear. Kenyon Lake and the tiny BCFS site sit central to the massive Douglas forest, high up over the east ridge above the north end of Stave Lake. This lake, situated in sub-alpine terrain at an elevation of 700 meters, is one of the few lakes of this height that you can get to reasonably easy with a vehicle. Kenyon sits on the dark north side of a high ridge, in an isolated U-shaped valley. Much of the time this traps fog and a cool dampness on the lake's surface creating a mysterious scene where you expect Excalibur to rise from the waters. This lake's reputation is based on good sized trout and the prolific flies. The camping site is very small but the many fishing tales told here are anything but small.

The mysterious look of Kenyon

FINDING the SITE This is a bit of a drama. First of all, because of active logging in the area, keep in mind the fact that roads can appear here almost overnight... they are everywhere. Secondly, it is a 33.6 kilometer haul from the intersection of Sylvester Road and Highway 7 in Hatzic. Since the road gets rough, you need at least a truck, preferably with four-wheel support for traction on the final rise. This is particularly true if your trip is early in the spring. It is definitely unsuitable for motor homes or cars. Also, because it is not easy to find this site, I really suggest you use your odometer.

Follow Sylvester Road through onto the Lost Creek forest service road. Pass Davis Lake at 18.5 kilometers, then keep right at 21.6 kilometers then left at 22.3. Cross Lost Creek and keep right at 24 kilometers. The road splits at the Salsbury Lake marker sign at 25.0 kilometers. Take the right branch and follow the east side of Salsbury Lake past the BCFS parking lot at 26.5 kilometers. Keep your eye on your odometer since things get a bit tricky from here. Keep driving straight through, ignoring the left spur road at 29.4 kilometers. Just a short distance beyond this take the left branch at 29.5 kilometers. This little spot is the site.

All is well until 30.6 where you need to turn left and start your descent into the valley. Cross the bridge over Terepocki Creek and turn left at 31.3 kilometers. Cross the bridge over Kenyon Creek at 32 kilometers and take the right branch up the hill at 32.2 kilometers. Don't despair, you're close now. Take the left turn at 33.6 kilometers and, as you get ready to climb again, you get a nice surprise! A small open gravel area magically appears.

SITE DESCRIPTION The site is a flat gravel area not more than 40 meters wide, the only open flat place in this area. It is positioned 75 meters away from the lake, near its outlet, skirting a small wooded area. The open gravel lot serves as camping and parking facilities. The biffy sits at the far end of the clearing. The site is large enough to accommodate four or five parties at most. A garbage can and a few fire rings mark where campers have cooked their enormous rainbows. From the camping sites, a good gravel trail heads through a wooded swampy area that slopes gradually to the lake only 75 meters away. Hauling a car-topper or canoe is easy enough along here. The shoreline has been cleared of brush making it easy to plop a small boat into the water. Keep in mind that the open parking/campsite is limited in size and you may need to park on the road. Don't worry about getting a parking ticket in this place!

SPECIAL FEATURES and ATTRACTIONS Kenyon Lake is a nice size at 26 hectares and reasonably deep. Its elevation of 700 meters makes

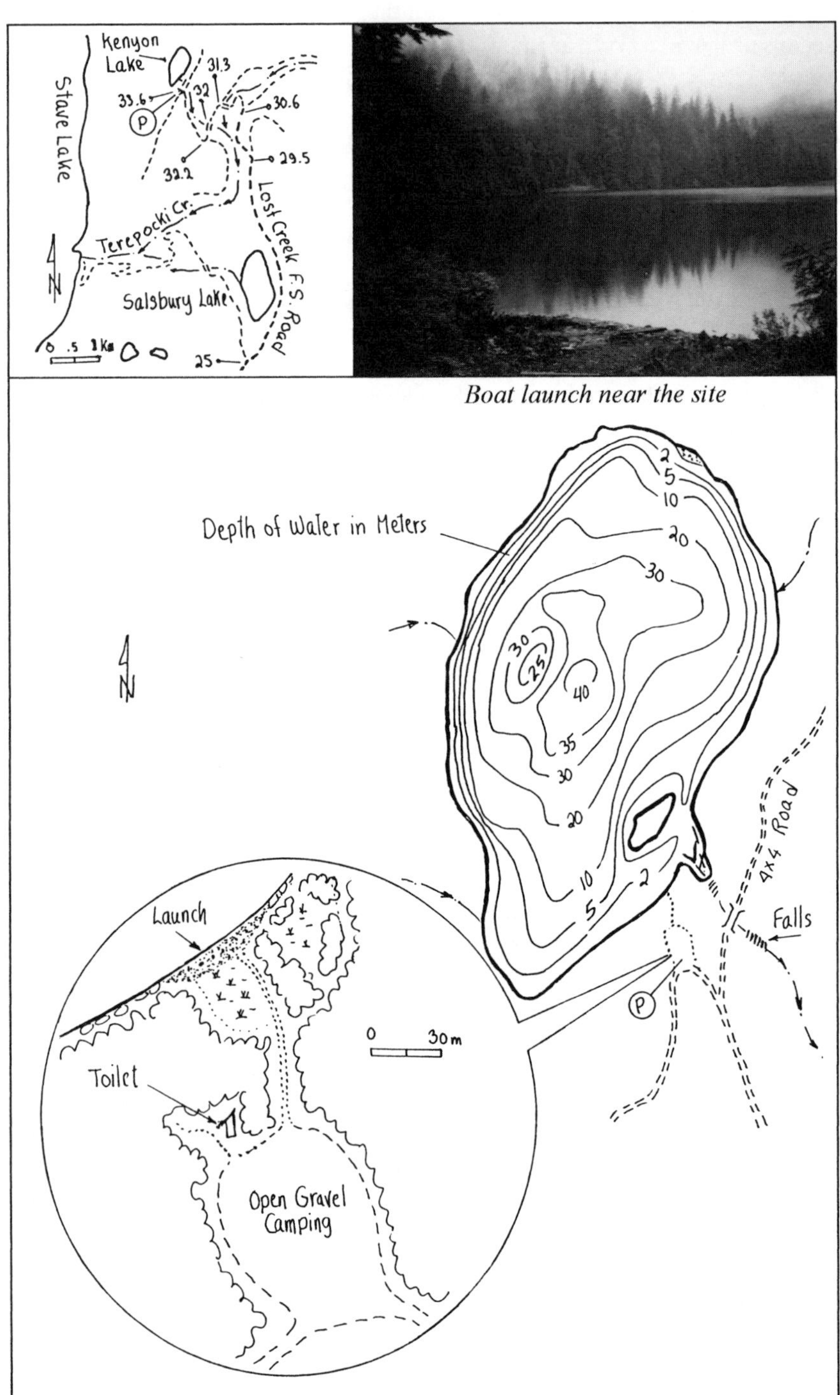

Boat launch near the site

its waters cool all year. Its sub-alpine qualities presents a picture that will make you hold your breath when you see it. It has a-mystical appeal. When you start climbing these wide goat trails they call logging roads you will hardly believe there is room for a 26-hectare lake up here. The shock of finally finding it is only surpassed by the shock of its raw beauty. When you finally park in the tiny little roadside campsite and walk to the lake, you will enter a unique scene of rugged beauty. The lake is set precisely between sharply rising rock slopes. The lake's waters, after resting placidly in this basin, then spill past the island thundering down the cliffs to meet Terepocki Creek far down in the valley.

Fishing This is one of those fly fishing paradises. The fish are well-fed by the vast fly population. Big hint... insect repellent is a must. Cool water and fighting rainbows are your target and this lake is quite deep compared to its neighbor Salsbury, reaching 40 meters in the middle. I have purposely included water depth contours for those interested experts. The little picturesque island is inviting but the water is shallow here. Stocking has been consistent since 1987, placing only a small number of 6,000 yearlings in the lake, but it probably doesn't need it.

Canoeing A canoe is a must. You can skim across these cool, clear waters and really appreciate the natural beauty of the area. This lake's setting of sub-alpine vegetation contrasted against a backdrop of craggy rocks and the sharply rising ridge of a U-shaped valley is sheer magic. The lake even has a little island. The clarity of the water will intrigue you and if you happen to be here on a still summer day, the scene will stay with you for a long time. The launch is just a small mud/gravel area that has been cleared of brush so don't expect much and you won't be disappointed.

Trail biking The surrounding area is networked with roads and creeks. Much of the terrain has been logged, some of it recently. This opens numerous exploration adventures. The map and the directions to the lake should have told you that the roads are everywhere. This is truly a place where the biker or 4X4 adventurer will get a chance to test mechanical partners and navigational skills. But be careful because many of the roads are not maintained. It's great fun to belt along on the bike but it's surprising how fast an unexpected washout dampens your fun.

TWIN BRIDGES 5

☑ FISHING
☑ TRAIL BIKING
☑ TENT CAMPING
☑ RECREATION VEHICLES

It is not intuitively obvious why this place was chosen to join the list of sites. Perhaps the unique convergence of three creeks is the highlight. A well endowed site this is not but it is the only formal place to park and camp in this maze of very rugged valleys and creeks. Named because of the two bridges that cross the split in the North Statlu Creek, this small site sits at the intersection of three creek branches converging beside the bridges. If you're a creek diddler, enjoy frolicking on boulders, love the rush of cool water and get off on the roar of rapids, park here for the night... you will not be disappointed. It is a very small site with few of the regular natural attractions but at times this in itself is the attraction.

Clean waters and endless boulders of Statlu Creek

FINDING the SITE To get to the site, take the Chehalis forest service road from Highway 7 at Harrison Mills. Turn left just past the Sasquatch Inn. The road has a good solid gravel surface with a few rough spots but you would be able to navigate this road with a car.

The main road is easily distinguished, but spur roads are plentiful and can be confusing. Stick to the main road heading north for 14.7 kilometers where you will encounter a major junction after crossing Statlu Creek. After pondering the clarity of the inviting pools in the creek, continue to the left. You will cross this creek twice more as you proceed west. Keep right after the first crossing. The left branch takes you to Margaret Pass and across to the Norrish Valley. If you are looking for views keep this road in your memory. At 22.2 kilometers you will approach a gravel parking area and see the two bridges crossing the split in the North Statlu Creek. The open gravel site on the other side of the two bridges is the BCFS site.

SITE DESCRIPTION The site offers three open places where you can park a vehicle or pitch a tent. And in this area, open spaces are rare. Two open gravel areas are large enough to park a camper. The center area is large enough for one camp site. There is a garbage can and a biffy at the main north site.

SPECIAL FEATURES and ATTRACTIONS The site itself is not too attractive in that it sits right on the main logging road and is subjected to dust. The convergence of the three streams at this point is, however, the feature. In the summer these creeks are not too violent and it is a nice place to cool off with a swim or fool around with a small rubber raft. The creeks tumble down wide bolder beds alternating between pools and runs... cool and refreshing. A few deep green pools may even offer a trout if you feel up to fishing.

Trail biking The main Statlu Road continues well up into the canyon, then a branch loops around to Dickson Lake. Another branch goes south through Margaret Pass to the Norrish Valley. This was noted in the directions. It takes you high up over the Margaret divide and down Norrish Creek to Dewdney. Yet another system proceeds northwest up Blacklock Creek. Then there is another extensive system penetrating deep up the North Statlu. Each of these has a set of their own branch roads that reach deep into every type of rugged terrain imaginable. These roads, found in various states of condition make a vast network to explore with a dirt bike or 4X4. Be aware that various states of road condition should be underscored. These roads change with the seasons. Most are not maintained and some are just downright dangerous.

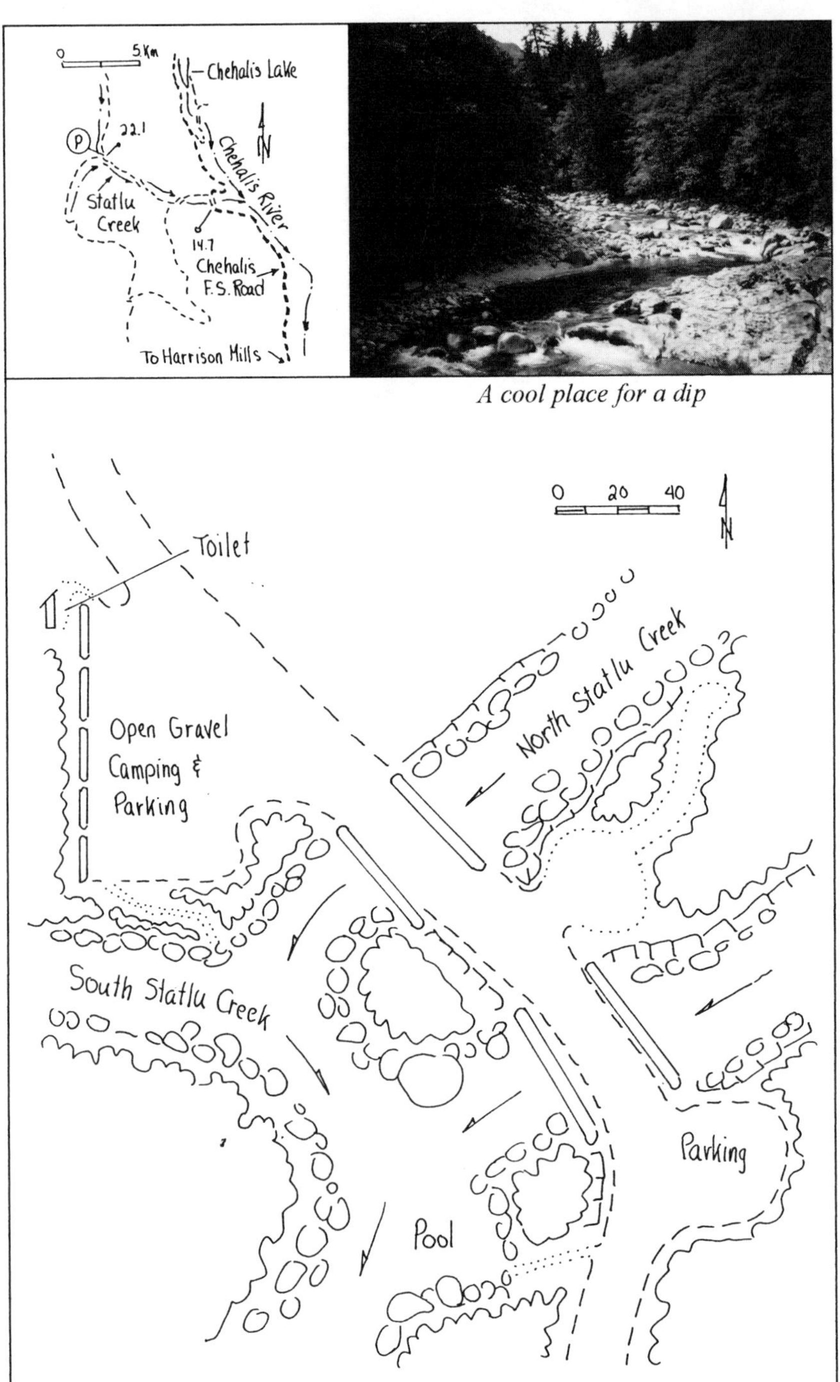

A cool place for a dip

CHEHALIS LAKE SOUTH 6

☑ CANOEING
☑ FISHING
☑ BOAT LAUNCH
☑ BOATING
☑ TENT CAMPING
☑ RECREATION VEHICLES
☑ MEDIUM SITE

There is only one word to describe Chehalis Lake... majestic. For so many years this lake has been limited to weekend access because of active logging. This has made it difficult for most city dwellers to consider this place as a serious recreational area so the vast majority of valley residents have never seen this spectacular valley. More recently the access restrictions have become more relaxed, placing unbelievable weekend pressures on the three BCFS sites on the lake. Chehalis Lake and the valley it sits in are big and beautiful, a true wilderness wonder. The setting is rugged and remote. Cleaner waters you will not find. If you take a trip up here you will really appreciate just how beautiful the area is. Chehalis Lake South is one of three BCFS sites on this massive lake. It is the official boat launch site for Chehalis Lake.

Chehalis River surges out of Chehalis Lake

FINDING the SITE Access to the site is from the Chehalis forest service road off Highway 7 at Harrison Mills, just past the Sasquatch Inn. The main road is easily distinguished, but spur roads are plentiful and can be confusing. Stick to the main road for 14.7 kilometers where you will encounter a junction just after crossing the Statlu Creek bridge. Continue to the right. Parallel the river to the east for a while, then turn north again and climb abruptly. At 19.8 kilometers, you will note a spur road dropping to the right.

To get to the Chehalis South, take this right access road. It quickly drops down into the Chehalis River canyon, then it crosses the river over one of the most spectacular fishing pools on the river. Cross the bridge and take the left branch that climbs abruptly up the slope. This section is not quite as good as the main road. It is rough and steep requiring a truck for clearance. It is unlikely that a motorhome will make this section. Once up the hill, the road eventually levels off and you emerge at the lake, a total of 25.8 kilometers from Highway 7. You should also note the left road to the main camping area before you approach the lake.

SITE DESCRIPTION The site extends along the south end of the lake forming a crescent shape around the east side of the bay. There are two parts to the site, one focused on the boat launch and beach, and the other closer to the bushy part of the bay's end, opposite the Chehalis River exit point. At the very end of the road you will find a good concrete boat launch designed to serve the entire lake for trailer-boat launching. This is a bit of a contradiction since it is not exactly easy to haul a good sized boat up the hill and maneuver it around the narrow road to the ramp. This marks the end of a narrow slightly sloping bench that yields to the cliffs and the water, converging at the ramp in a narrow parking area. This area has limited flat ground so there are not a lot of campsites here. They are distributed along the shoreline back from the ramp, where at lower water levels mid-summer the sandy beach appears along this strip.

The less popular but formal pads are found back from the launch area at the end of the lake where the water forms a large bay before it plunges into the canyon. If you recall the left spur road a short distance back, it accesses a loop road that reaches the tip of the bay. There are about 10 formal camp pads distributed along this loop but vegetation is thick. You will find the odd picnic bench, garbage cans, and a central biffy here.

SPECIAL FEATURES and ATTRACTIONS Chehalis Lake has to be the most incredible lake in the area. It is very large at 629 hectares, set in the rugged wilderness of the Chehalis Valley. This lake will boggle your mind when you first see it—long and thin, measuring about ten kilometers long, it is only an average of one kilometer wide.

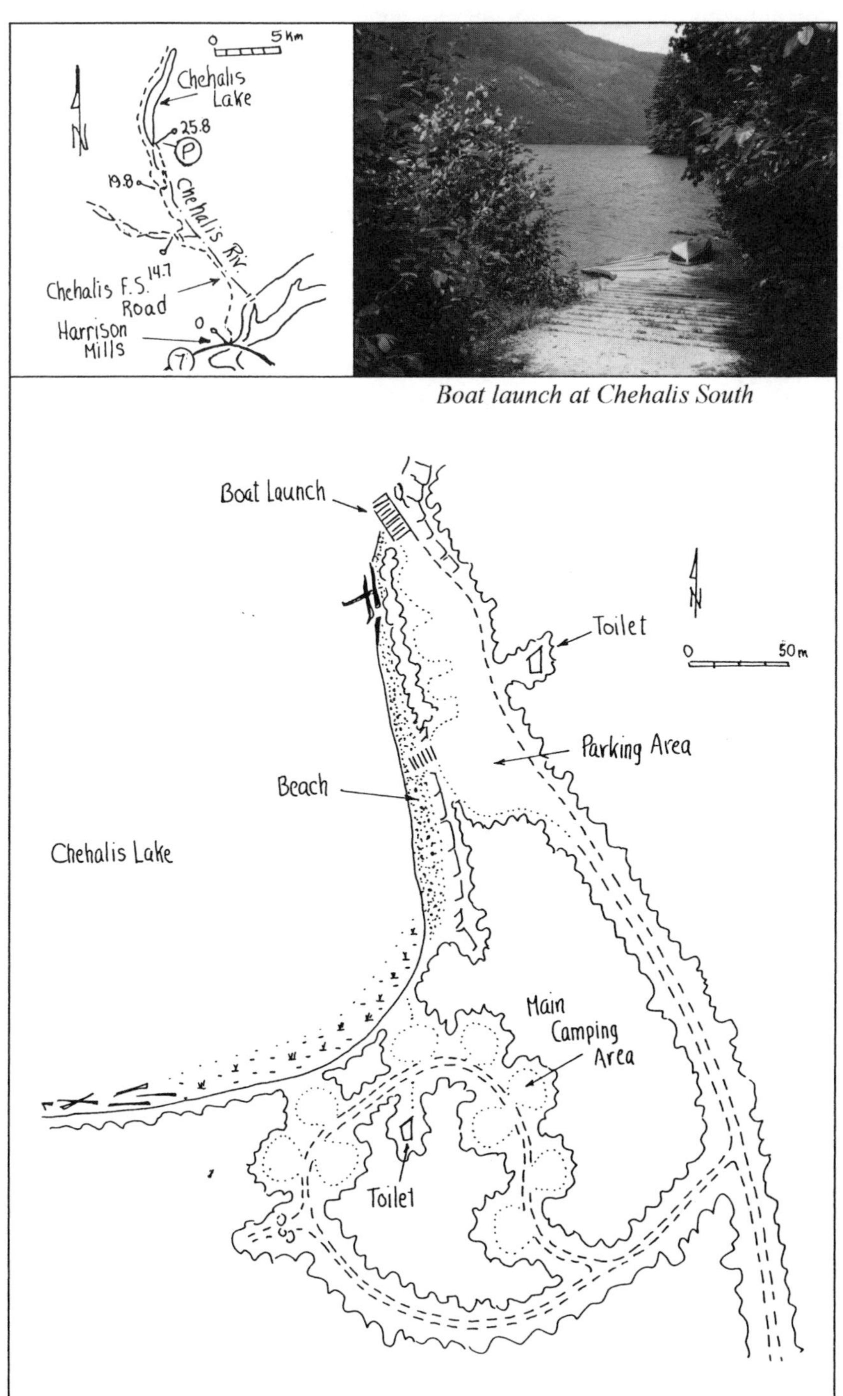

Boat launch at Chehalis South

Literally squeezed between Mount Fletcher and Mount Orrock on the west and Mount Downing on the east, the lake sits at an elevation of 227 meters, low compared to the towering peaks that rise to well over 1200 meters. The lake is well circulated by a multitude of powerful streams. The mighty Eagle River enters at the north while Skwellepil Creek pushes rocks into the west side. Chehalis River exits to the south. Along the ten kilometer stretch of shoreline you will find at least another twenty streams pouring into the lake.

Boating Without a doubt, this lake is a boating paradise because it is so large and so clean. The shorelines dip quickly into the crystal-clear water, reaching depths of 150 meters mid-lake, providing a totally-unbelievable shoreline to explore. The multitude of streams, steep cliffs, secret sand bars and untouched shore vegetation provide an almost unending variety of shoreline features to interest any boater. And because of the thin width, it is easy to head for shore in foul winds. Winds do get strong since they have a good chance to build velocity as they surge through the valley, with little resistance from the smooth lake. On a calm summer day this massive body of water can be totally placid but white-caps are not uncommon when the wind picks up. If the vessel you depend on is small, stay near the south end. It is somewhat protected from the winds.

Fishing It would be difficult to talk about Chehalis without mentioning the fishing. It provides a natural habitat for large dollys, rainbows and whitefish. The lake is extremely deep, particularly at mid-lake where it reaches depths of 150 meters. One of the favorite spots is at this south end where it shallows gradually to ten meters just before it spills over into the canyon, forming the spectacular Chehalis River canyon. Reports of five-kilogram dollys taken on fenders and worms are common. This end of the lake is protected from harsh winds, making it excellent for canoeing, trolling and even fly fishing. As another fishing bonus, the river itself is famous for Steelhead and the pool at the bridge should have already enticed you if fishing is your passion.

Trail biking This area is a vast network of back roads, most of them abandoned and very rough, providing a great opportunity for hiking, 4X4 exploring and dirt-biking. Most of the roads offer spectacular views of some of the mountains and valleys. Local to this area, a vast network opens up if you get back to the Chehalis River bridge. To the south the Fleetwood forest service road heads back down the east side of the Chehalis River. To the east, up Maisal Creek, an almost endless network of roads head deep into the valley and up to 1400 meters in elevation around Mount Davies and Mount Downing. The best map to use is the Fraser Valley 1:100,000 scale map published by World Wide Books and Maps in downtown Vancouver.

SKWELLEPIL CREEK 7

- ☑ BEACH
- ☑ CANOEING
- ☑ FISHING
- ☑ BOAT LAUNCH
- ☑ BOATING
- ☑ TENT CAMPING
- ☑ SWIMMING
- ☑ HIKING
- ☑ TRAIL BIKING
- ☑ LARGE SITE

Skwellepil Creek is the most impressive recreation site on Chehalis Lake. It is one of the more impressive sites in the BCFS list. The second of three BCFS sites on Chehalis Lake, this one is found at mid-lake, on the most appealing spot on the lake. A large, flat, tall-timbered gravel bar has been formed at lakeside pushed out by the crystal clear and forceful waters of Skwellepil Creek. In summer, the exposed gravel beach, the clear waters of the tumbling creek, the park-like setting and the shady camp site overlooking the glassy water of the lake combine to form one of the recreational highlights of the valley. If you have never seen this area, an excursion to this place is a must, particularly if you can do it away from a weekend. It will clearly illustrate the raw beauty in the Chehalis Valley. You will not regret the trip, despite the 30 kilometers of dust.

Looking south from Skwellepil Creek

FINDING the SITE To get to this site, take the Chehalis forest service road north from Highway 7 at Harrison Mills. Just as you pass the Sasquatch Inn take a left, zero out and travel north on the gravel road. This road has a good solid gravel surface with a few rough spots but there are no steep inclines that would require a four wheel drive. The exception is the last .5 kilometers that drops off the main road to the site. It can get chewed up by 4X4 traffic making it tough for a car.

The main road is easily distinguished as you head north. Stick to it for 14.7 kilometers where you will encounter a junction just after crossing the Statlu Creek bridge. Continue to the right paralleling the river east for a while, then turning north again and climbing. At 19.8 kilometers, you will note a spur road dropping to the right. (Note that this is the access road to the main boat launch at the BCFS Chehalis Lake South site).

At around 24 kilometers, you will begin to see the lake as you have risen high above it. Continue enjoying views of the lake until the 30.1-kilometer mark. You will see a spur road angle back and down steeply. This short road of 500 meters will dive down the bank to the site then flatten as you approach the lakeshore. If your vehicle is a car, park at the top and walk down for a look first. I definitely do not recommend taking your Viper down here.

SITE DESCRIPTION The lakeshore slopes gradually into crystal clear green water, opening up a panorama of lake-mountain scenes between the large conifers that completely cover the area. Most of the space is open with no underbrush, allowing you to pitch camp or park just about anywhere. At the shore the gravel-rock beach drops quickly into deep green waters and it is along here that you find a complex network of open, natural, wooded campsites although they are not formally demarcated as pads. These set nicely in the trees, many of them allowing a cartop boat to be launched from your backyard. There is also an open gravel area that serves as a boat launch. The area is serviced with biffies, garbage cans as well as fire rings and even picnic tables.

Back from the beach there are several other open areas that serve as camping pads. These are just as nice, set in the shade but away from the beach. Another fantastic area for camping is along Skwellepil Creek at the north end of the site. Along here there are a few more bushes to give a bit of privacy. The prime ones sit on the bank of the creek where you can hear the rush of the water. It is near here that the creek enters the lake forming a large gravel bar perfect for sunning or fishing... what a combination!

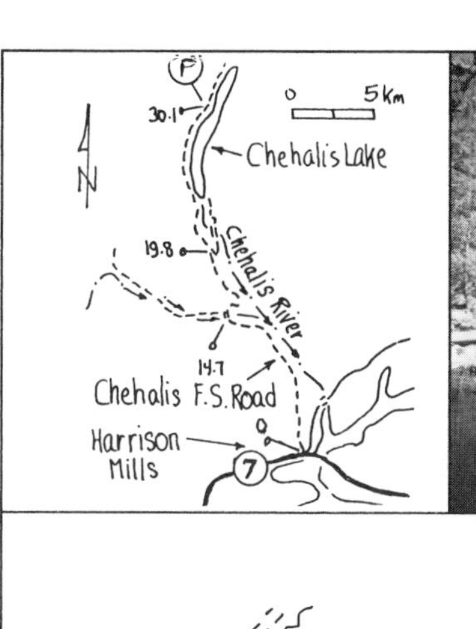

Fishing hole at Skwellepil's mouth

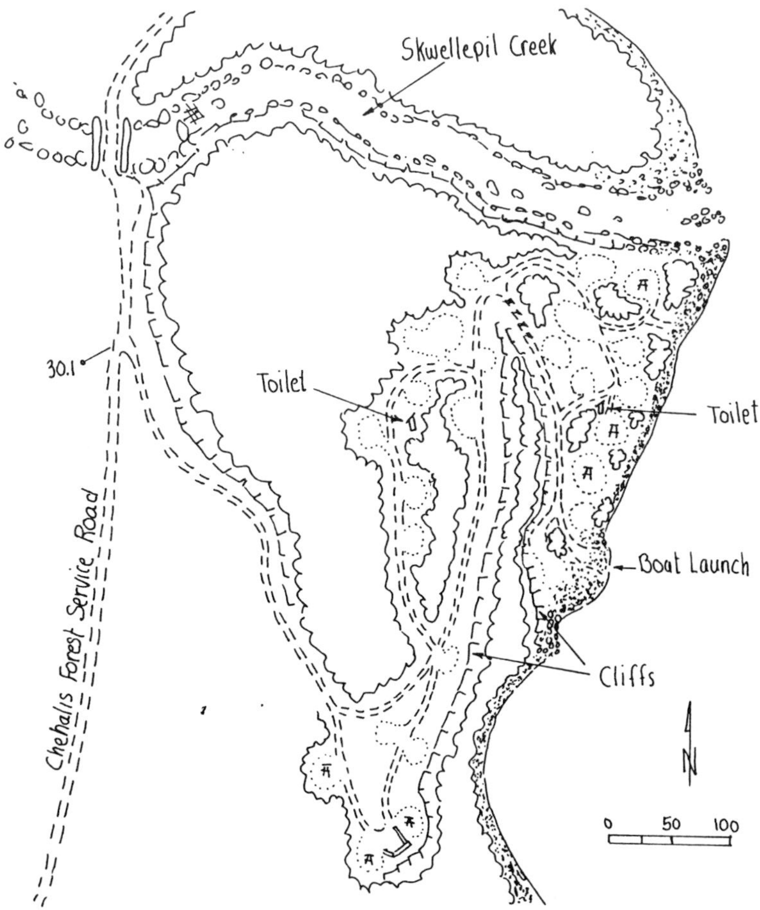

Skwellepil Creek
30.1
Toilet
Toilet
Boat Launch
Cliffs
Chehalis Forest Service Road
N
0 50 100

SPECIAL FEATURES and ATTRACTIONS There are many attractions in the Chehalis Valley area, the main one being the lake itself. To keep from repeating these I have tried to cover the extras found *only* in the immediate area of the site. You should read about the Chehalis South and Chehalis North sites covered before and after this site.

Boating This lake is a boating paradise because it is so large and so natural. If you have a larger boat and trailer you should consider using the ramp at Chehalis South. At this site there is no official ramp but nevertheless it is possible to launch a smaller vessel off several pads. Here the shoreline slopes gradually, then dips quickly into the crystal-clear waters providing access both north and south to a totally unbelievable shoreline of gravel bars, rocks and cliffs.

Hiking and trail biking This area has a vast network of old roads, most of them abandoned and very rough, providing a great opportunity for hiking, 4X4 exploring and dirt-biking. Most of the roads offer spectacular views of some of the surrounding mountains and valleys. Just opposite the road down to the site there is an extensive network of roads that reach deep up the south side of Skwellepil Creek then up Middle and Gerty creeks, high up to Mount Fletcher and Wilson Lake. The old road up to Wilson Lake is almost 4 kilometers long reaching a fantastic destination near the lake. Another road system follows up the north side of Skwellepil deep into the valley. It ascends high up into some spectacular scenery. None of these roads are in good shape so dirt bikes and boots are your best option. Pack a lunch and head up to Wilson Lake, you won't forget it.

Fishing The lake provides a natural habitat for large dollys, rainbows and whitefish. The lake is extremely deep, particularly south of the site where it reaches depths of 150 meters. To the north of the site it reaches a mere 100 meters. Skwellepil Creek has pushed a massive amount of gravel out in this area forming a divide in the lake. In this particular spot, a large gravel bar has formed at the mouth of the creek. From this projection the water drops cool and deep to a bench. This is one of the better spots to troll or spin off the boat.

Swimming The gravel beach area and the tumbling waters of Skwellepil Creek offer a cool place for a swim in summer. At this time, the mighty waters of the creek slow down to roll over large round boulders forming crystal green pools and rolling rapids. Opposite the camp pads, the creek is about 30 meters wide, offering many dipping spots. The interesting thing about this is that the creek steepens upstream quickly, getting more turbulent, changing from placid rolls at the bottom to falls near the upper road. Thus the choice as to challenge and degree of turbulence is yours... a super place to frolic with a rubber raft.

CHEHALIS LAKE NORTH 8

- ☑ BEACH
- ☑ CANOEING
- ☑ FISHING
- ☑ BOATING
- ☑ TENT CAMPING
- ☑ RECREATION VEHICLES
- ☑ TRAIL BIKING
- ☑ LARGE SITE

Another spectacular site on Chehalis Lake, this third BCFS site is situated at the north end of the lake. This one has been formed by some violent natural forces, changing the site's look every year. The North Chehalis River and the Eagle River combine their forces north of this point to push an unbelievable quantity of material into the lake. The result over time has been to force mountains of huge boulders, gravel and sand out into the lake forming a large flat area that has mostly grown in with timbers. Along the river bank you can see enormous boulders and logs strewn for a hundred meters laterally before they get pushed into the lake during the next run-off. The force of the river emptying here has also maintained a 90 meter deep hole in the lake at the mouth. Yet other forces such as the wind and turbulent eddies have surged endless trees and logs into the north west end. All this comes together to create a very unique, placid site in summer.

The rugged boat launch at Chehalis North

FINDING the SITE The site is accessed by following the Chehalis forest service road north from Harrison Mills just past the Sasquatch Inn. It is possible to drive a car to this site if you are not afraid of potholes and 34 kilometers of dust. Drive on this main road for 14.7 kilometers where you will need to keep right after crossing the Statlu Creek bridge. Continuing along the right fork you will parallel the creek to the east for a while, then turn north again and climb up above the lake elevation. At 19.8 kilometers, note a spur road dropping to the right. This is the access road to the Chehalis South BCFS site and the official boat launch.

At the 30.1-kilometer mark, you will see a spur road angle back and down steeply to the second BCFS site at Skwellepil Creek. Continue along the main road and you will eventually drop down to lake level again to encounter the turnoff to the Chehalis Lake North site at 33.4 kilometers. This road cuts back along the west shore forming two loops back around through the tall trees as it reaches the lake.

SITE DESCRIPTION The whole area is mostly rocks, boulders and gravel. How the large grove of conifers have managed to grow here is a tribute to their survival abilities. Fortunately, this makes a nice shady setting for the many camp pads that are distributed along the river as you enter the site and also at the head of the lake. As you enter the site, many pullouts have been beaten by Goodyear to form pads on the river bank. Farther in, as you approach the end of the lake, the nicest spots skirt the gravel-sand beach area - if the water is low. The road then curls around back to the main road along the river, offering several other pads.

There is another more secluded section looping off the main loop. These pads are much rougher but close to the lake. During lower water you will get either a massive tangle of logs and debris, or a nice open beach... it all depends on what the winter forces decided. The winter winds like to gather momentum up the lake, also blowing logs and trees onto the shoreline in this area, so even cartop boat launching can be a challenge.

There are ample campsites (about 40) set in the natural timbered surroundings, many along the shoreline. The popularity has increased quite dramatically, however, so don't get too excited about the number. Biffies, garbage cans and picnic tables can be found distributed through the area. At low water the beach is fantastic, at high water there isn't one. If you need to launch, it is possible to do so at the two prime sites found on the shore between the two main loops (see the site layout map). Otherwise a haul through the trees with your weightlifting friends is the option.

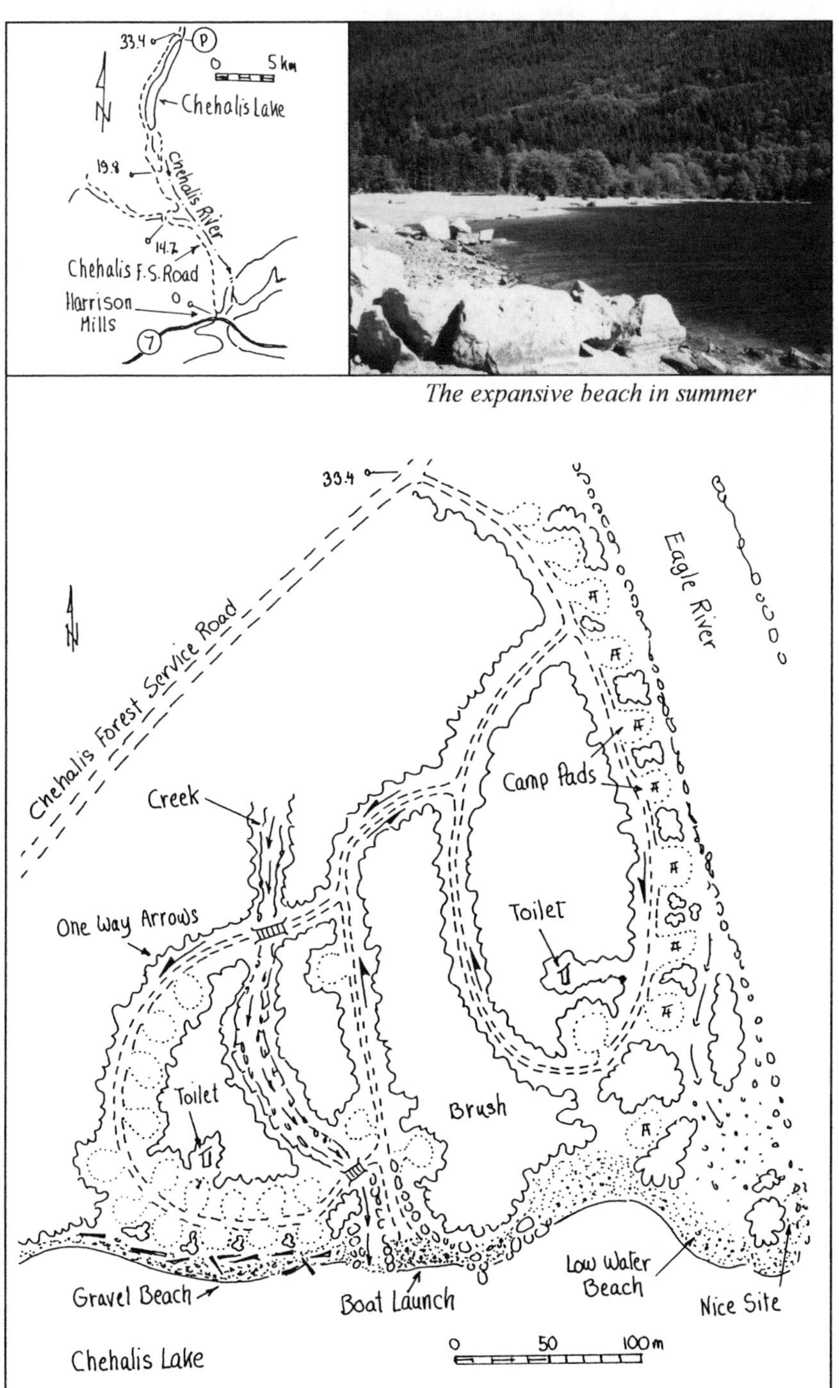

The expansive beach in summer

SPECIAL FEATURES and ATTRACTIONS There are many attractions in the Chehalis Valley area, the main one being the lake itself. To keep from repeating these I have tried to cover the extras found *only* in the immediate area of the site. To get a complete picture, you should read about the Chehalis South and Skwellepil Creek sites covered earlier.

Boating Although the official boat launch is found at the south end of the lake, it is still possible to get a small boat in the water here. Parking is a problem here so don't get too excited about taking a large trailer. The shorelines typically dip quickly into the crystal-clear water providing a totally-unbelievable shoreline of rocks, cliffs and gravel bars to explore. Along the lakeshore at this end there are many good sized streams that tumble and crash down the cliffs into the lake, excellent places to fish or cool off.

Fishing The lake provides a natural habitat for large dollys, rainbows and whitefish. The lake is extremely deep, particularly at mid-lake where it reaches depths of 150 meters, so fishing the shoreline is usually the best tactic. Of particular note is the deep pool at this end of the lake south of the beach. It reaches a staggering 90 meters of depth in a short distance off shore. The mouth of the Eagle River is another popular spot to fish and then there are five main, and many smaller streams, crashing down the mountain in the general vicinity.

Trail biking This area is a vast network of back roads, most of them abandoned and very rough, providing a great opportunity for hiking, 4X4 exploring and dirt-biking. From the site there are several long road systems. The continuation of the Chehalis forest service road takes you deep into the Eagle River Valley. If you cross the bridge over Eagle River, this system will take you north then east through the Sasquatch laden Mystery Valley across to Harrison Lake. Along each system there are endless spur roads to explore.

CHEHALIS RIVER 9

☑ FISHING
☑ HIKING
☑ RUBBER RAFTING
☑ RECREATION VEHICLES
☑ KAYAKING
☑ TENT CAMPING
☑ RIVER SWIMMING
☑ LARGE SITE

For so many years this special place on the Chehalis River was known only by a small group of locals and used mostly by ardent Steelhead anglers. Through their many years of pursuit they beat an extensive footpath along the Chehalis River atop canyon walls, finding uncanny ways to climb down to the many deep green pools. So intense was the plight that there is hardly a spot on the river where a pool escaped them, even though the deep gorge cut by the river exhibits sheer rock walls 50 meters high in some places. One example of the canyon is found at the BCFS site just as the river makes its final surge out into the open valley.

The spectacular Chehalis River Canyon

Now this famous Steelhead river has lost its secrets but the staggering beauty, and the unbelievable trail still exist. BCFS has artfully carved three fantastic camping areas here creating a place where an endless stream of new visitors play every year. If you stay here, try spring or fall and prepare for an unforgettable hike.

FINDING the SITE Leave Highway 7 at Harrison Mills just past the Sasquatch Inn, or take the Hemlock Valley-Weaver Creek turnoff before the Inn. Either way, both converge at the start of the paved Morris Valley Road a short 200 meters in. The Morris Valley Road continues along the valley floor skirting the Harrison flood plain until you cut inland to finally reach the Chehalis Bridge at 5.7 kilometers. Stop before crossing the bridge. At this point there are three choices. The *southwest* recreation site is found by turning right along the gravel road before the bridge. It has a yellow gate across the road which disappears rapidly into the trees. A small *northwest* site is found along the left bank of the river before the bridge, accessed via a short road to the left. The *northeast* site is found by turning left after the bridge.

SITE DESCRIPTION Once the Chehalis River finishes with its run through the canyon it settles down into a steady run through a wide gravel rock channel all the way to the Harrison River. The BCFS site is spread out on either side of the wide channel on the gravel banks that have formed from the power of the river. The main road and the Chehalis bridge cut over the river close to where the river comes out of the canyon, splitting the site into three distinct recreation areas, each with their own unique characteristics.

The *northeast* site is found after the bridge on the left, strung along the river bank. It has a gravel parking area, with several camping pads situated on the river bank and also several pads along the right side of the road situated in the shade trees. The short road ends at a large open site and the start of the trail up the rock bluff into the canyon. There are garbage cans, a few tables and two biffys set in the trees. This site gives the best access to the canyon since it is next to the trailhead and the first deep pool at the foot of the cliff.

On the *northwest* side there are fewer spots but these are all very nice, situated in the trees on the bench overlooking the river. There is also a biffy servicing the area and several cans for garbage. If you drive in a short distance you will come to a large secluded open area perfect for a larger recreation vehicle. The road terminates here but a footpath continues to the mouth of the canyon.

The *southwest* site is the largest, offering at least 25 superb camping pads distributed in a loop skirting the river and then around through the tall trees. This area is particularly heavy with hemlock and fir trees towering upwards to block out the sun completely. Underneath this thick canopy, the terrain is flat with no underbrush, presenting a magic, park-like setting within easy access to the river. Several biffys are central to the loop and many of the pads have picnic tables. Fire rings are common. The nicest area is the large open spot at the

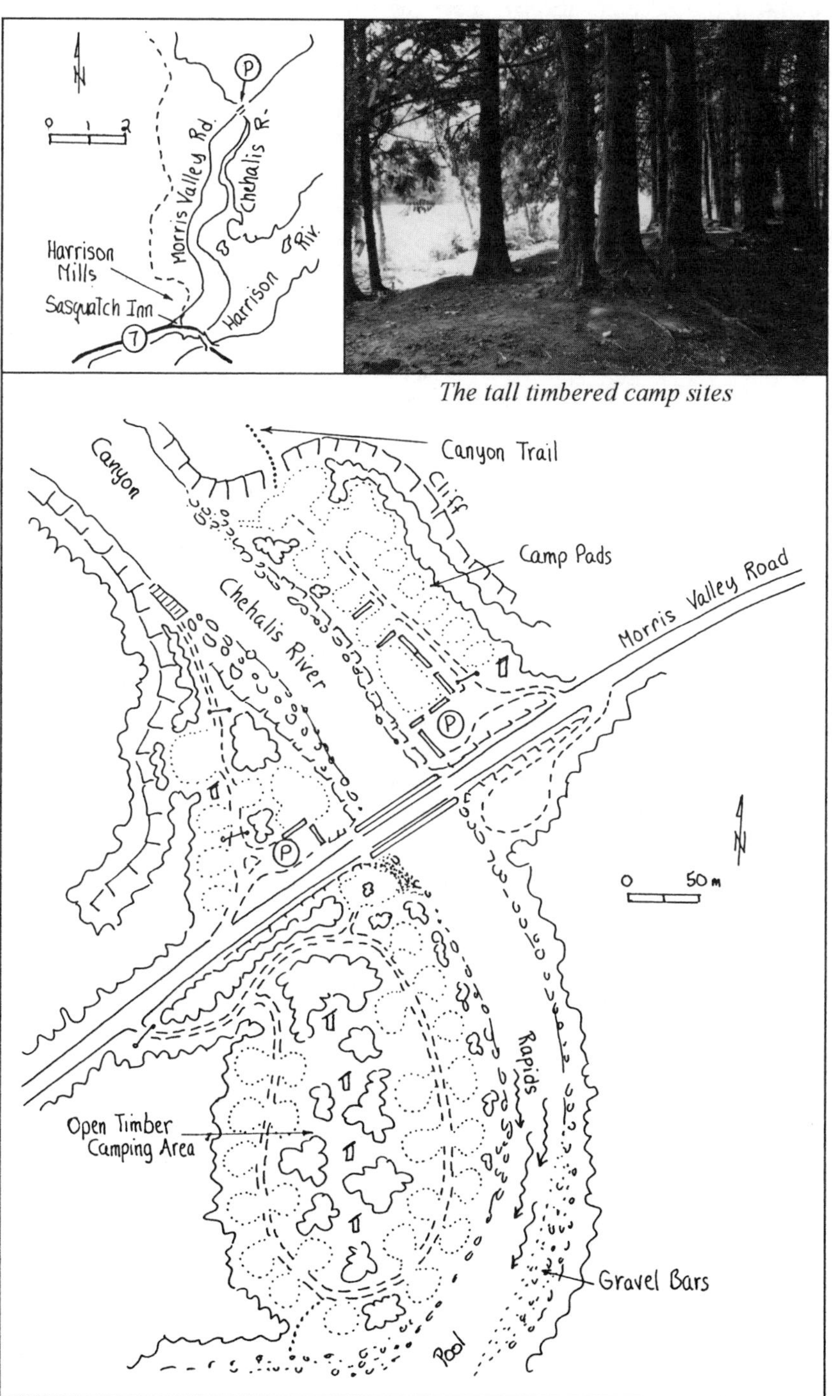

The tall timbered camp sites

north of this section, directly under the Chehalis bridge. There is a private sandy beach here and the site is large enough to take several families.

SPECIAL FEATURES and ATTRACTIONS

Chehalis River Canyon Trail Dominating this region is a rugged quality landscape cut sharply by the furious river. Along the top of its cut, which in many cases is vertical for 50 meters, are groves of pine, hemlock, cedar and fir trees, some giants reaching a few meters thick. The trail follows along the top of this deep cut. As you hike through this magic setting you catch unbelievable views of deep, green pools, joined by rushing rapids and perfectly clean gravel bars that snake along the sides of runs. In many places the rock wall drops straight down disappearing in the deep emerald water. If I was a fish it would be difficult to leave this place.

The trail starts at the end of the northeast site, climbing straight up the canyon and beyond for several kilometers. The discouraging part is the start since it doesn't waste time getting to the top of the cliff. You climb rapidly to get a bit of a fright when you look down a sheer drop to the deep green pools below, 30 meters down. The trail skirts the lip of the rock wall to enter the woods and emerge again at another spectacular pool. This sequence becomes common as you alternate from rapids to deep pools, each viewpoint along the cliff more spectacular than the last. Each sequence presents a gravel bar in a snake-like sequence. At each pool you will find some form of steep path taking you down to the gravel bars. These drops are not designed for Granny. You usually have to scramble down the rocks to the river. But once on the river, you find many exceptional spots to fish in season and stop for a cool swim or a picnic. Each year this trail gets punched a little farther up the canyon.

It is reasonably easy to visit three magnificent pools, each requiring some sure-footed balance to descent down to the water's edge. The trail thins, climbs and drops along steep rock walls before it really gets tough. At that point you need to have a bit of mountain goat in you to continue.

Rubber rafting If you like to fool about with a rubber raft there are two choices. The upper run is made of a sequence of rapids and pools that vary in degree of white water depending on the season. In winter an expert would shy away from this place. But in summer this changes to give any rubber raft lover an exceptional place to frolic since the river is less violent. To try your skills, you need to hike up the river as far as you feel compelled, climb down to the pool and take the run down all the way to the deep gorge close to the site.

The lower run, from the bridge to the pool below the south camping area is also a great run but much more sedate and shorter. The shallower water is perfect for an air mattress in summer. At other times of the year, the river surges through here making it a challenge for even the more adventuresome whitewater enthusiast, or kayaker. This run is short and if you take it, consider stopping at the pool at the first bend then looking ahead before your next run. In this section the river has a tendency to change its course every year because it accumulates huge piles of logs and debris ripped out of the canyon. These act as a dam dispersing water violently in every way through the tangle. These are excellent places for slurping you under logs if you are not paying attention.

Fishing The fishing opportunities in this river should not go unmentioned. For years this has been one of the best Steelhead fishing rivers in the valley. There have been some large ones taken here. In fact, the river canyon trail was originally beaten out by Steelheaders heading up the canyon to catch their dreams. The trout, salmon and Steelhead opportunities are fantastic, but regulations change so check first. Alternatively you can head down to the Chehalis Fish Hatchery. The fish hatchery is found a short distance before the Chehalis bridge. Here you can have a look at the salmon hatchery and walk down to one of the most popular fishing spots on the river. A trail skirts the hatchery taking you down to the Chehalis River, just above where the main channel comes into the hatchery.

WEAVER CREEK 10

- ☑ CANOEING
- ☑ FISHING
- ☑ BOAT LAUNCH
- ☑ BOATING
- ☑ TENT CAMPING
- ☑ RECREATION VEHICLES
- ☑ HIKING
- ☑ MEDIUM SITE

It wasn't so long ago that a trip to Weaver Lake was an arduous 2 kilometer trek along an unforgiving road. So it used to be a favorite place for hardy fishermen and sturdy 4X4's. Now, with the improved road, the Weaver Creek site, set on the southern shores of Weaver Lake, has become a favorite family place. It has become one of the recreational highlights of this area because there are several exciting attractions for the fisherman, canoer, hiker, or camper. Set in a remote basin of picturesque Hemlock Valley, this site is endowed with good facilities, good trails, is reasonably easy to access and it presents a vast wilderness playground where it is possible to satisfy many recreation tastes.

Still waters at the south end of Weaver Lake

FINDING the SITE Access is via the Morris Valley Road, which you must take from Harrison Mills. Take a left turn past the Sasquatch Inn and zero out if this is your first time in the area. Then take an immediate right onto the paved Morris Valley Road. At 11.3 kilometers from the highway, as you pass the Weaver Creek fish hatchery drive straight through onto the Harrison West forest service road. This will lead you to the Weaver forest service road found at 12.7 kilometers. Weaver Lake is another 2.4 kilometers up the hill so your odometer would read 15.1 when you arrive at the lakeshore. This is usually a good gravel road with a few rough spots so a truck is your best bet early in the season. A high-slung car will make it through the summer. A few rough spots will be encountered with some rapid gains in elevation. When you reach the lake you will be at the southeast corner. If this is your first time here, drive to the left up to the Weaver Creek bridge. Most of the lake is actually hidden from this viewpoint. From the bridge you will be looking up a narrow segment that looks like a small channel. This is the only boat access point to the water.

SITE DESCRIPTION The site is spread around the south east extension of the lake where Weaver Creek exits, central to the entry road. This is the main lip of the huge basin containing the lake. When you approach the lake, be aware there are two campsite areas and a day use area. When you first drive in you will note a parking area to the right where the short 100-meter road ends in the trees. Water access is poor around this side because of a log cluttered-mud dominant shore. The lake is shallow on this side, typically cluttered with logs and debris. This serves as the parking and also marks the southeast end of the Denham's Trail surrounding the lake. A toilet has been placed here to service the hikers.

The main day use area and larger parking is found to the left, around the Weaver Creek bridge where the creek flows out from the lake through a channel cut into the rock. A gravel roadway just to the right of the bridge slopes gradually to serve as a small boat launch. It is reasonably easy to back in a small trailer. A biffy is central to the area and several day use pads with picnic tables and fire rings are distributed around this area. The setting is picturesque, overlooking the quiet, placid section of the lake.

Past the bridge are several open camp areas along a small creek. They are set in the woods away from lake water. Most have a picnic table or remnants thereof. A biffy is also central to this area. Most facilities at the lake are well-organized and well maintained with several open gravel areas large enough to park a camper or trailer. Several picnic tables are available, along with the usual garbage bins, and fire pits.

Alternatively, if you feel it is necessary to escape from the crowd you can pack up and hike around the other side of the lake (or paddle across) where there are several open gravel beaches on the other side... but no facilities. Here a nice open area overlooks a deeper drop-off section of the lake.

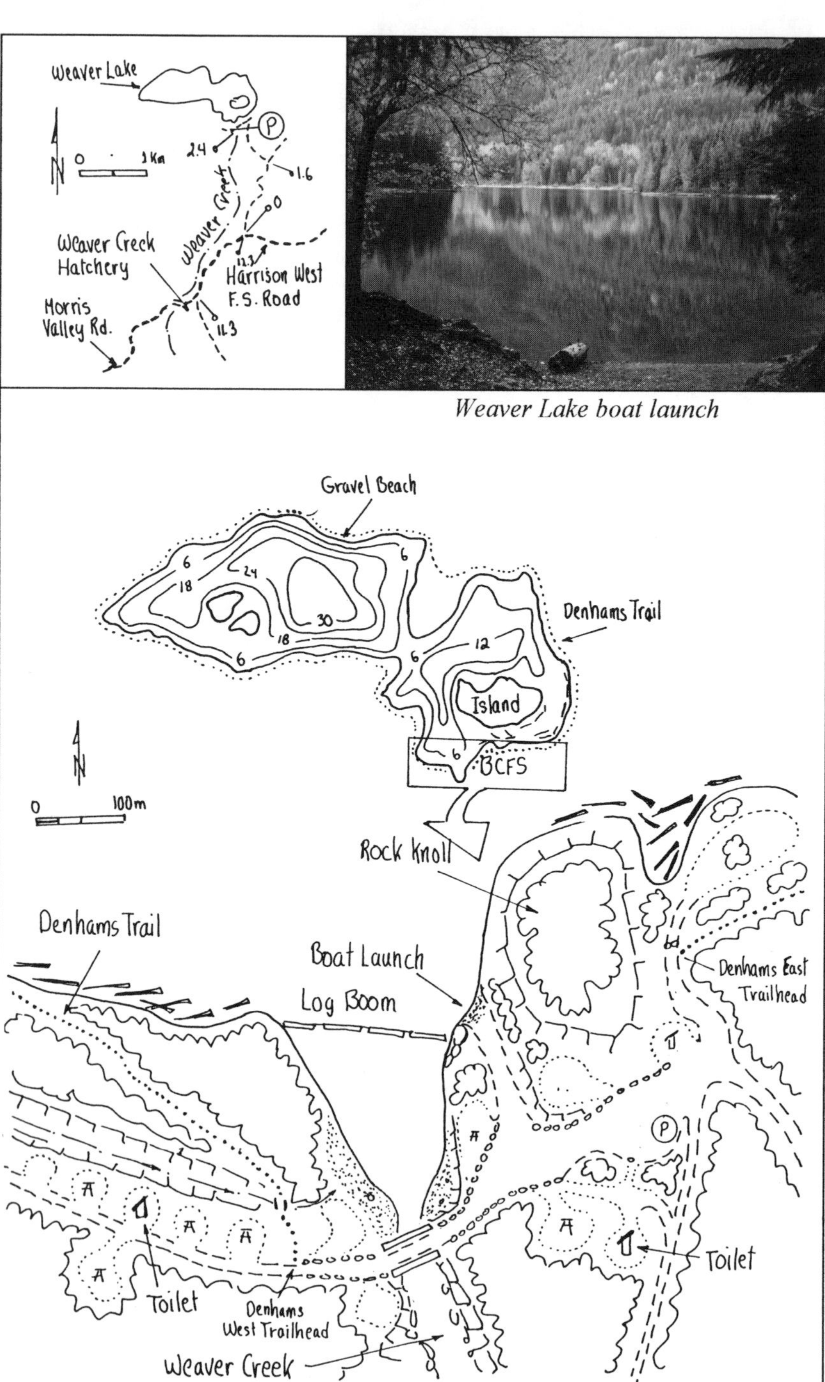

Weaver Lake boat launch

SPECIAL FEATURES and ATTRACTIONS Weaver Lake is the absolute highlight of this area. It is a beautiful lake of 81 hectares set in the thick, lush forested valley below the Hemlock skiing area. Low in the valley at an elevation of 258 meters, the lake is completely surrounded by a lush carpet of forest. The lake setting, its decent size, interesting shoreline and cool clear waters combine to give this area a unique, unparalleled beauty. For years this has been a special place to fish and boat; 50-centimeter rainbows being the prime reason. A distinctive feature of the lake is that it has several islands to add to its character, offering a wide variety of interesting shorelines, coves and channels to explore. In addition, an extensive trail system has been developed around the lake perimeter offering terrestrials endless areas to explore.

Boating and Fishing The lake is a fantastic place to take a canoe because of the variation in the shoreline. The valley is also well-protected from harsh winds. The fishing is good and it is easy to spend the day exploring the lake. The north beach area is particularly quiet and peaceful if you want to stop for a picnic.

Fishing at this lake is a quality experience, particularly with a boat. The shoreline is not easily accessed at the south end, much of it being muddy and log-strewn so you pretty well need a boat to get out there. The fisheries have been stocking Weaver Lake with rainbows since 1986 at a rate of 6000 yearlings each year until 1990. You can typically expect fish around 30 to 40 centimeters. But many reports of 50-centimeter fish make the lake even more of an enticement to a fisherman.

A close look at the lake shows the east part is relatively shallow, dominated by sunken logs and debris that have blown in from the other side. The deeper waters are to the right as you pass the first island and then to the west as you pass into the main lake.

Denham's Trail Although the south shore is not too accessible, the Denham's Trail provides many opportunities to reach the water if you are prepared to walk a bit. The Denham's Trail takes you right around the lake. The southwest trailhead starts just past the bridge and takes you all the way around to the east trailhead. The walk is 6.2 kilometers with little elevation gain, taking three to five hours depending on how many times you stop to ponder nature or fish. Around the west end of the trail you can reach a couple of good viewpoints strategically located on some rock thrusts.

The trail is fairly easy to walk and is well maintained. Much of the eastern section of the trail takes you through a wide variety of vegetation hugging the shallow log-cluttered shoreline. Since it stays close to the lake much of the distance, you can get to the shore easily to cast your line out. On the north side just before the rock bluffs, the shoreline opens to gravel and the water dives quickly off shore. This is an excellent place to stop, even camp or take a cool dip. This is where you can roast a weenie and fish.

The northwest section of the trail is different in that it skirts the rock bluff on its march back into the woods to the west. Here the trail has some new bluffs to skirt at the west end of the lake. It is only a slight gain in elevation, enough to get a bit of a view of the lake. From here the trail hugs the shore and the dense bush all the way back to the recreation site.

GRACE LAKE 11

☑ CANOEING
☑ FISHING
☑ TENT CAMPING
☑ RECREATION VEHICLES
☑ SMALL SITE

The Grace Lake site is a cozy quiet little place with easy access. Situated 12.9 kilometers northeast of Harrison Mills, this little spot is squeezed between the main Harrison west logging road and the small Grace Lake. The main attraction is the picturesque little lake which is very inviting to any one with a floatation device and a fly rod. This place is small, supporting only a few campers but it is purposely designed this way to limit stress on the delicate ecosystem. Once you park off the road and get a glimpse of the area, the beauty of the lake and its natural pristine shoreline become obvious. It is a perfect place to park a camper, put up a tent and try out the new canoe.

Grace Lake's shallow shoreline

FINDING the SITE Finding this site is fairly simple since you can see it from the main Harrison West forest service road. A car is adequate for the whole trip. From Harrison Mills at Highway 7, proceed north a few hundred meters past the Sasquatch Inn, then turn right on the paved Morris Valley

Road. Continue past the Weaver Creek fish hatchery at 11.1 kilometers, then drive straight through onto the Harrison West Road at 11.3 kilometers. You would continue straight through at 12.7 kilometers, passing the Weaver forest service road and start up a small incline. Just as you start the climb, at 12.9 kilometers there is a small open area to your left. This is the lower section of the BCFS site set beside the exit creek. From here the small trail cuts over the creek and follows the shoreline around the west end.

The second and larger site is just another 50 meters farther along the road. You can pull off and inspect the facilities. From here access to the lake is easy since the lakeshore is just 20 meters from the cleared area.

SITE DESCRIPTION The forest service has carved a small campsite area into the tall trees right beside the road with room for about five or six campers or tents. Much of the area contains rock outcrop dotted with timbers, clear of underbrush, presenting a park like setting beside the lake. There is an upper and lower section with the old familiar green biffy standing like a lighthouse, perched on the rock beside the parking area between upper and lower pads. There are a few picnic tables and some garbage cans in the area. The topmost spot is the largest of the two but the area is subject to dust from the nearby traffic. If you want to appreciate this place, forget about getting a spot on a weekend. There just isn't a lot of space here so try it mid-week. Access to the water is easy since the site sits on the lakeshore. Since the road is made of a hard gravel surface, it is easy to park a camper or recreation vehicle here. Resist any attempt to park a Winnebago here or you may find yourself scorned by your neighbors.

Adjoining the lake on the left the open gravel area is more protected. There is a rock outcrop on the lakeshore which offers a bit of hard ground, a commodity rare on this side. From this main site you can launch a cartop or canoe using two short pathways. These consist of a short walk to the muddy lakeshore. The other requires a short climb over rocks near the stream exit from the lake. Since the shoreline is only 20 meters from the sites, the process is reasonably easy even though there is no formal launch.

The smaller camp pad area with a lonesome picnic table is just below the main site to the left. This is a nicely cleared area set under the trees and beside the little exit stream, making it a rather refreshing spot. A small footbridge straddles the creek to a small impressive setting of mossy rock outcrop. Some shade trees and a few bushes set strategically to hide you and yet present a nice open view of the lake. Just behind this is a little stream babbling its way over the outcrop. You are virtually on lakeshore here, a very scenic, relaxing setting to pitch a tent but the area is small and not able to support more than one camper.

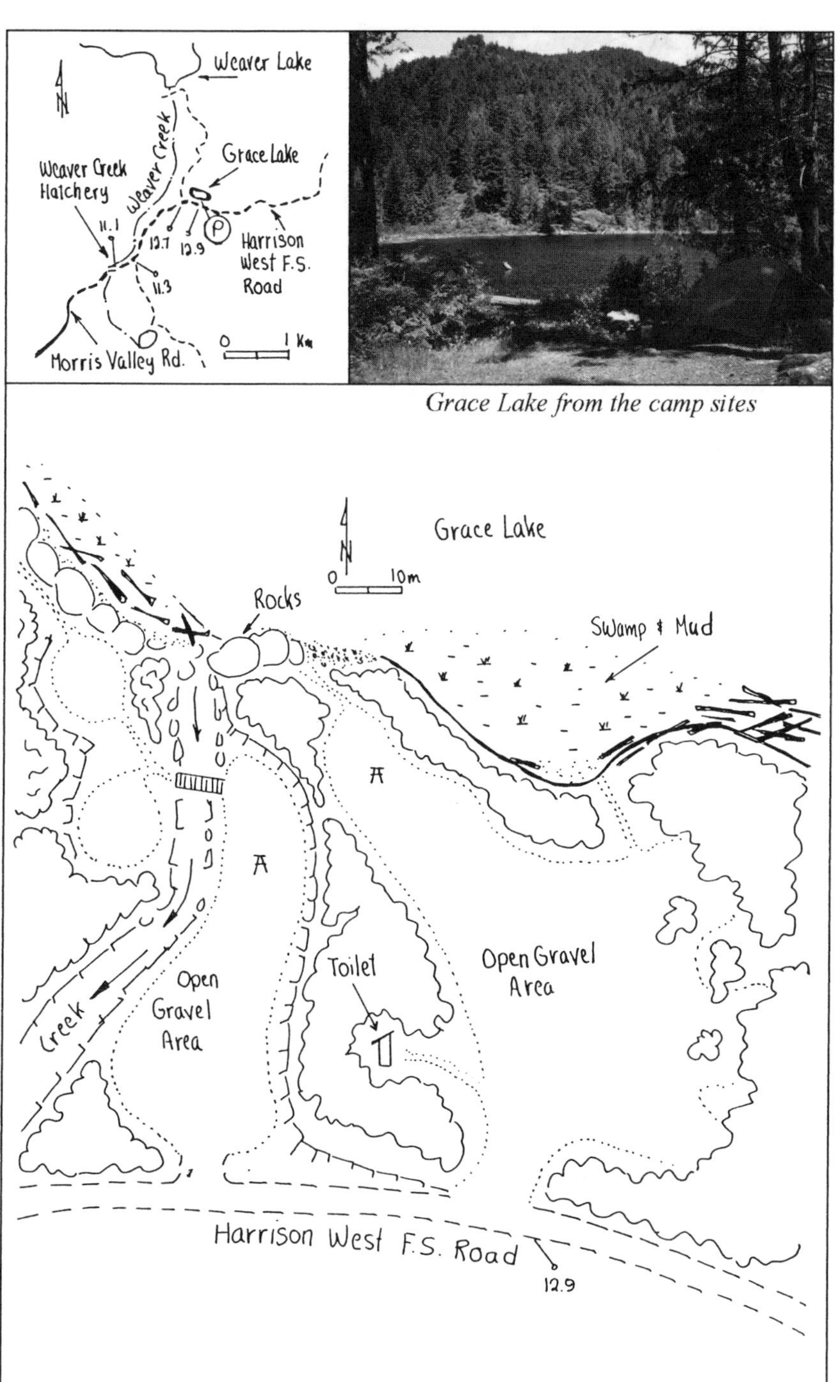

Grace Lake from the camp sites

SPECIAL FEATURES and ATTRACTIONS Grace Lake will remind you of a large swamp at first sight. A fair number of logs and debris have accumulated along a shallow muddy shoreline. At the west end the lake spills its water through a small stream, slipping quietly down the rock outcrop area, central to the campsite. Creating a rather picturesque setting despite the debris, Grace Lake is a 'cozy' lake of six hectares, sitting invitingly in the flat, forested plateau area at an elevation of 106 meters. The chosen recreation site offers tall shade trees, rolling rock outcrop and open areas facing the lake. Since the lake is shallow around the perimeter, the shoreline is commonly mud and marsh making access somewhat challenging if your goal is to keep your boots on.

Fishing restrictions have been placed on this little lake to protect it. This includes no power boats, making a great place for a canoe or a rubber boat. Reports indicate that 30-35 centimeter rainbows are taken quite consistently, probably because of the stocking program which has placed at least 6,000 fish in this lake.

Note that the BCFS marker sign indicates that this is *Wolf Lake*. This is incorrect and does not correlate with fisheries information or the Energy Mines and Resources topographic maps. For some reason this lake is confused with the next lake just up the road.

WOLF LAKE 12

- ☑ CANOEING
- ☑ FISHING
- ☑ SMALL SITE
- ☑ TENT CAMPING
- ☑ RECREATION VEHICLES
- ☑ VIEWING

This site should take the record for the smallest BCFS recreation site on this side of the valley. The site is literally squeezed between a rock knoll and the drop-off to Wolf Lake's shore. Like its little neighbor Grace Lake, Wolf Lake is also a tiny body of water but it is much less exposed. Hidden away in a heavy forested hole bordering on an extensive swampy ecosystem, the lake is virtually inaccessible except through the tiny site. Yet for those lucky enough to get a spot here, the illusive rainbows and placid waters of the lake offer a very special place to relax. But dry, clear space is at a premium and it is not easy to turn around if the site is crowded so try it off weekends and you will really appreciate it.

Wolf Lake, a perfect place to cast a fly

FINDING the SITE From Harrison Mills at Highway 7 take a turn left just past the Sasquatch Inn and proceed north a few hundred meters to turn right on the paved Morris Valley Road. Continue past the Weaver Creek fish hatchery at

11.1 kilometers, then drive straight through onto the Harrison West Road at 11.3 kilometers. Continue straight through at 12.7 kilometers, passing the Weaver forest service road and start up a small incline. As you start the climb, at 12.9 kilometers take a quick look at the pretty Grace Lake and continue slowly. As you level off at 13.1 kilometers you will see a spur road on your right, marked by the familiar brown BCFS sign (as Grace Lake).

The spur road is only a short .5-kilometers long but it is a narrow roadway with one rough spot that will require a truck or a car with good clearance so taking a motorhome in here is a definite no-no. As you approach the lake you will see it glistening through the tall fir trees in a gully about 20 meters down the bank to the left of the road. A short distance farther and you will come to a small narrow clearing overlooking the lake. This narrow plateau is it!

SITE DESCRIPTION The road dead-ends at a small grassy clearing overlooking the lake which doubles for the camp pads. The small cleared area is not designed to support hoards of campers so don't think about being too picky about a spot. From here there are a couple of footpaths cutting sideways below the bank to lakeshore, about a 15-meter drop below the parking area. Two or three parties will take over the whole area. Since this is a rather narrow plateau squished between the rock bluff above, the drop-off to the lake and the swamp, there is not a lot of room to spare. Nevertheless, you will find a few picnic tables, a garbage can, a hidden biffy guarded by giant mosquitoes and a few fire rings.

The setting is pretty and peaceful, positioned on a bench overlooking the lake. The site is about 15 meters above the lake. A short footpath switchbacks down the bank to the shoreline where you could carry your car-topper or canoe. There are other trails taking you down to the exit stream and one of the large ponds. A trail to a choice view above the campsites has also been beaten out.

SPECIAL FEATURES and ATTRACTIONS Wolf Lake is the feature attraction here. Set in a hole at an elevation of 106 meters, the setting is interesting, with a heavily wooded west side and a large open marsh around the rest of the lake. At a mere two hectares in size, the lake is small, with more swamp along its south shore than the lake area itself. The swamp area is another 4-6 hectares reaching southwest into the valley of marsh, obviously the work of some industrious beavers. This provides an abundant food supply for the larger fish inhabiting this little lake. The main lake is fed by a small stream from the north. The exit is to the south. Although limited in space, the place still offers an angler, camper or canoeist a nice, quiet opportunity to relax and try a hand at some excellent fishing.

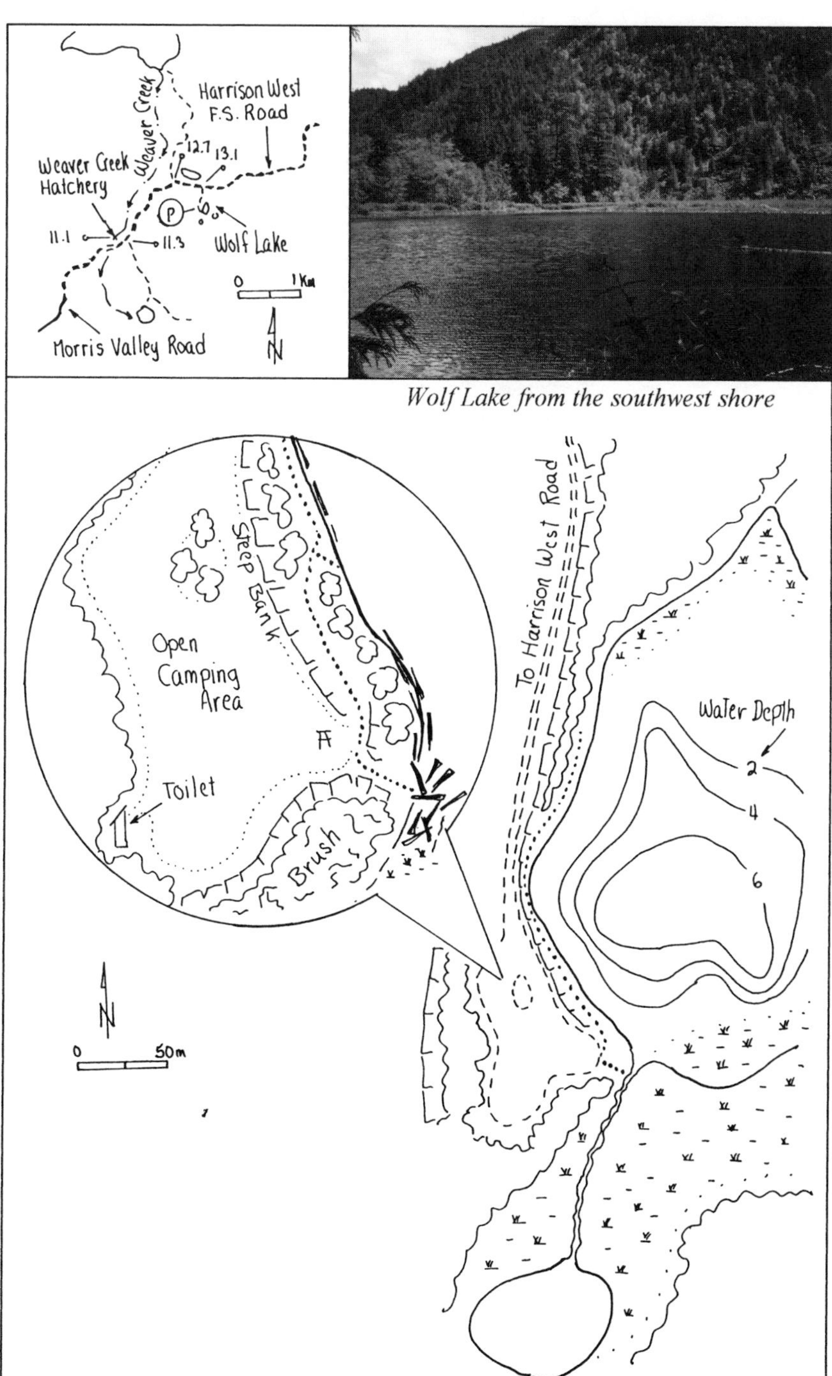

Wolf Lake from the southwest shore

Fishing The lake has been stocked with Rainbow yearlings since 1986. The program is not as aggressive as Grace Lake but the lake is quite small. At any rate, if those yearlings have avoided the angler's barbs since 1986 they are too big to swim out of the creek! The lake is very well-protected from winds so a belly-boat is a perfect device to try here. Shore fishing from the campsite side is difficult since the vegetation on the bank makes casting awkward. The south trail leads to the mouth of the exit stream where it is possible to cast out, but shore fishing is essentially tough. The open marsh area just on the other side of the exit stream is directly over the deeper bank so if you can manage to push your way through the brambles, that is the place to try casting.

The lower trail under the bank below the site is slowly being extended by heavy boots around the lake, beaten a little farther each year. By now it may even get you around the other shore. There is only one restriction for this lake: no power boats. Not surprising for its size.

Note that the BCFS marker sign at the road indicates this is *Grace Lake.* This is incorrect and does not correlate with Fisheries information or the Energy Mines and Resources topographic maps. For some reason this lake is confused with the lake just down the road.

FRANCIS LAKE 13

- ☑ CANOEING
- ☑ FISHING
- ☑ HIKING
- ☑ TENT CAMPING
- ☑ BOAT LAUNCH
- ☑ SMALL SITE

The attraction here is that this site is not yet an attraction. The small recreation site sits beside tiny and rugged Francis Lake, 366 meters up on a rather isolated divide, overlooking the Harrison River Valley. This site has not yet become too popular because the road to it is not that good, its initial approach is steep and sometimes rough depending on the season. The few kilometers of steady climbing keeps most city dwellers and their Porsches away. The best way of picturing this place is by imagining a picture of a belly-boat fantasy fishing hole, rough and rugged, never touched by a fly rod. It requires a bit of an effort to get there but it offers an excellent fishing-camping excursion.

From the boat launch at Francis Lake

FINDING the SITE To get to the site, take a left on the gravel road past the Sasquatch Inn and then turn right on the paved Morris Valley Road before Harrison Mills. Proceed northwest to get onto the Harrison West service road just past the Weaver Creek fish hatchery. You will pass the turnoff to Weaver

Lake, then climb past Grace Lake and pass the Wolf Lake turnoff at 13.1 kilometers. Continue along this road northeast until you catch magnificent glimpses of Harrison Lake. The road follows the lake at a fair elevation above it giving you spectacular views along the way. At the 19-kilometer mark you should be driving under the power-line and note a spur road marked as Harrison West-Francis forest service road, rising abruptly up the mountain on the left. This road is not meant for cars and a 4X4 or truck is suggested, particularly in the spring. It is not as rough as it is steep, so if you thought the main road gave you a good view of Harrison Lake, wait until you take this one! Toward the end of summer, the road is literally worn smooth by Goodyear so the drive gets easier until the rains start.

From the Harrison West road it is 4.4 kilometers to the lake. As you climb up the hill, you will encounter the Hemlock spur at 2.2 kilometers, but keep to the left and keep the faith—there really is a lake up here. At 4.4 kilometers along Francis Road, after a flat jaunt through the pass, you will finally reach a forest service sign. The right short fork takes you to a small opening overlooking the lake and an open area where camping is possible. The left fork takes you to the lower end near a few other sites where you can launch a boat. From here the road curves up and around to dead-end at the viewpoint and what is used as overflow campsites.

SITE DESCRIPTION The recreation site is right at the end of the lake, distributed along the eastern shore along the road. At the first entry point, you will find an open area about 40 meters across, beside the shore. A 4X4 trail of about 50 meters long plunges down the rocks to the spot where the trees have been cut for firewood. The area will support a few camp sites but not much more. At this point it is possible to launch a canoe or cartop along the muddy shoreline but this is not the formal launch. Back from the sign, the road continues to the south end of the lake, first past a wooded campsite on the left, across from the lonesome biffy, then past a small gravel launch opening at the end of the lake. Just another 50 meters will take you to a few other campsites, the best one at the creek exit near the south end. This is a very pretty spot beside the stream on the edge of the cliff, before the creek plunges into the valley.

There are only about 5 formal camp pads by the lake. If you need to find some extra space, there are two "overflow" areas. You can follow a beaten footpath back up the east side of the lake to a nice wooded area that is open and secluded with no underbrush. This is not a formal spot and camp fires should not be considered because of the dry moss and proximity to trees. To offset the secluded benefit, however, the brush is hostile and protective of the lakeshore. It is shallow here, muddy and almost impossible to fish from shore. There is also an open gravel area at the end of the road. These are the 'view sites,' perched on the top of the cliff, big enough to support two or three trucks.

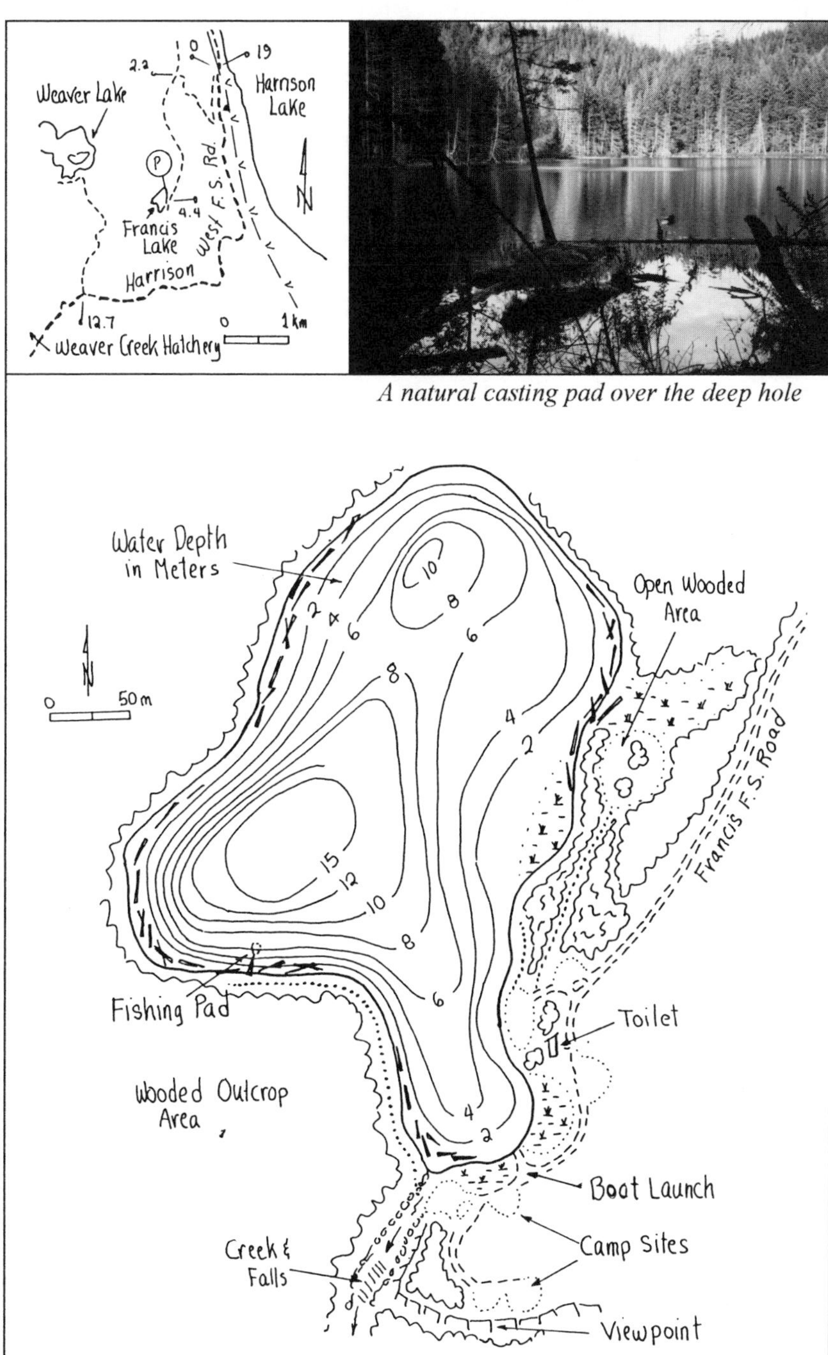

A natural casting pad over the deep hole

SPECIAL FEATURES and ATTRACTIONS This is a small site situated in a true, rugged wilderness setting. Francis Lake is the main feature, a small, round lake with a difficult, cluttered, brushy shoreline but quite well protected from wind since it is set in a basin. At four hectares the lake is limited in its capacity to facilitate many visitors but this is not yet a popular spot. The odds of finding a pad are decent, especially mid-week. Francis is quite isolated compared to its neighbors and is well worth a trip if you have not been into this area. It is picturesque and the air is cool and clean. There are also some spectacular views of the valley.

Fishing is primarily for smaller rainbows of around 30 to 35 centimeters but these are cool water fighters. The stocking program started in 1986, with 500 yearlings being placed in the lake until 1990. No power boats are allowed on the lake. There are two deeper holes in the lake, both on the opposite shores, the deepest taking you down to 14 meters. The south hole is accessed by following the footpath into the woods from the south campsite. A clump of roots sits just above the hole so it is obvious why the trail is here!

WOOD LAKE 14

☑ CANOEING
☑ FISHING
☑ BOAT LAUNCH
☑ TENT CAMPING
☑ RECREATION VEHICLES
☑ MEDIUM SITE

This pretty site is not quite as secluded as its neighbor sites at Sunrise and Francis lakes making it a very popular place on a summer weekend. This lake sits in an open, flat, rolling rock outcrop area de-nuded of any underbrush. The site is dominated by tall timbers to the north and smaller second growth to the south but nature has had a way of balancing this with rock and water to form one of the prettiest pictures in the valley. The lake is small but typically reflects a deep blue color, sparkling like a jewel in summer. It offers some decent fishing for its size and a magic place to camp. As a matter of fact, the place is so postcard looking, I decided to use it for the cover of the book.

The best camp pad on Wood Lake

FINDING the SITE To get to Wood Lake you can use your car but be prepared for a lot of dust. Heading east along Highway 7 at Harrison Mills, turn north (left) past the Sasquatch Inn onto the gravel road and turn right onto the paved Morris Valley Road 200 meters in. Now drive all the way to the Harrison

West forest service road. It continues through just past the intersection at 11.3 kilometers (past the Weaver Creek salmon hatchery). The Harrison West forest service road is a good all-season gravel road. Now you drive 20 kilometers more trading spectacular views of Harrison Lake for the dust. If you set your odometer back at Highway 7, you would read 31.3 kilometers before you saw the first access road to the south BCFS site at Wood Lake.

This first access road to the site is just a short half-kilometer drive to the parking area at lakeshore, looping around via the left branch. The straight-through branch on the right takes you to some 'overflow' campsites. To get to the other BCFS site (with the boat launch) drive a short .2 kilometers farther up the main Harrison West service road to 31.5 kilometers, then turn right to drive a short .3 kilometers to an open gravel area that doubles as the boat launch. The lakeshore is easily accessible from these two points, with well-beaten pathways found around sections of the lake.

SITE DESCRIPTION The small semi-open areas have been developed into two BCFS campsites, one on each side of the lake. Both areas have a toilet each and open campsites scattered about, mostly beaten flat by boot traffic. The north side of the lake is particularly pretty, offering open rolling outcrop, tall trees and no underbrush all the way to shore. The north site is the official owner of the boat launch. It is the open gravel parking area that adjoins the water. Since the lake is out in the open, you can easily find a spot to pitch a tent almost anywhere around the perimeter in this area.

The south area is not as well endowed with space, offering only a few select pads on shore. These are near a unique sphagnum moss hole—keep away from there or you may lose more than your boots! From the south parking area there is a bit of a path that curves around behind the moss hole and emerges at a neat knoll overlooking the east shore of the lake. It's only about 200 meters from the parking area. If you can live without your vehicle and want seclusion, try this spot.

There is a third "overflow" area to the far south created by fishing squatters who have worn the area open with 4X4's trying to get down to the stream.

SPECIAL FEATURES and ATTRACTIONS Wood Lake is the main attraction here. It is much different than the other lakes in this area in that it is much lower and easily accessed by car. It sits at 167 meters in elevation, close to the main road.

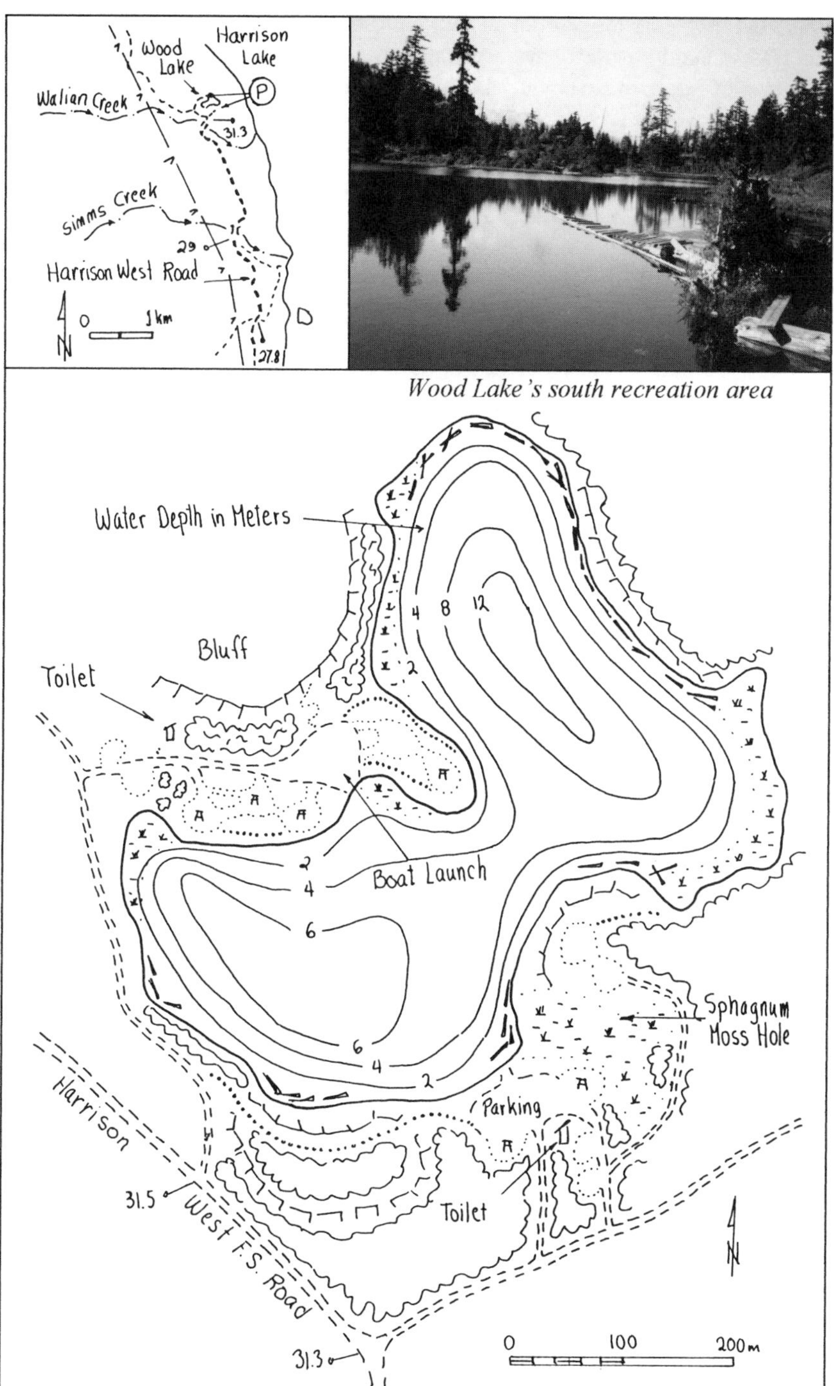

Wood Lake's south recreation area

Since the area was logged not so long ago, the place is sparse of trees. Small conifers and cottonwoods have taken over to give it an almost alpine look. The lake is split into two parts with a thin connector channel between the two bodies of water, squeezed by rocky knolls on each side. Mostly open, the area allows tents to be plopped anywhere, and with the exception of a few debris cluttered sections, the shoreline is easily accessed. Not surprising, the area has become very popular and despite its size of five hectares, it supports a vast crowd of campers in the summer.

Fishing The big surprise here is the fishing. There are some bigger rainbows in this lake. It is well-fed by streams rich in algae and has a deep hole on one side. It is well-protected, snuggled nicely in the knobby rock humps providing a really nice place to plop a canoe and fly fish for those 40-centimeter fish. No power boats are allowed on the lake, making it even more of a perfect spot for canoeing with fly rod. There is a footnote, however, in that this is not a very quiet spot mid-summer. You may be more likely to catch a spectator on shore or a float tube in the water than a fish. If you ever catch one in the summer you will have the rocks immediately covered with cheering spectators to support your efforts! The deepest area is actually in the northern portion of the lake, diving to a spectacular 12 meters in the middle! This may not seem like much but, given the size, this is relatively deep and perfect for trout.

The lake has been stocked since 1986, with the Fisheries placing about 500 yearling in the waters each year. This is by no means an aggressive program but the lake obviously doesn't need help. Reports are that the fish range in size from 24 to 40 centimeters and the prospect of a 40-centimeter rainbow on a fly is pretty hard to pass up. Be aware, however, that these big beauties are here because they are well fed and smart. If fishing is your main attraction be aware that this lake has become very popular in the summer so if you want to fish peacefully, try early spring or late fall. They bite better anyway!

HALE CREEK 15

☑ BEACH
☑ CANOEING
☑ FISHING
☑ TENT CAMPING
☑ SWIMMING
☑ BOATING
☑ SMALL SITE

When we first came down the hill to spot this rare secluded cove on the western shores of Harrison Lake, all I could say was "wow!" As we started to explore the fringes of the cove, the excitement of the prospects of camping here became overwhelming. Elegantly integrated into the large trees between Hale Creek and the sandy-gravely cove, this small site is one that you would prefer to keep secret. Such places on this lake are rare and it is even more rare to find easy access, despite its 4X4 requirement. Historically this site has been listed as *boat only access* but you can get in by 4X4, or a short 2 kilometer hike.

The pleasant camping pads at Hale Creek

FINDING the SITE To get to the site you can use your car if you plan to hike the last 2 kilometers down the hill to the lakeshore. Otherwise you need a 4X4 to get you down to the site. The site has been listed as a "boat use site" so there is no marker on Harrison West road for vehicle visitors. Recently, one leg of the circular road down to the lake has been improved making vehicle access a bit easier than before.

First, let's get to the area by 4X4. From Highway 7 at Harrison Mills, just past the Sasquatch Inn (heading east) turn left (north), then right onto the Morris Valley Road driving all the way to the Harrison West forest service road. It starts just past the intersection at 11.3 kilometers (past the Weaver Creek salmon hatchery) as Morris branches right. The Harrison West forest service road is a good all-season gravel road. There are many spur roads off this main road and you need to drive 36 kilometers along it. If you have never been here swallow your pride and set your odometer at Highway 7. Your first major warning will come when you hit the Hale Creek bridge at 35.2 kilometers then take a sharp turn right to encounter the Hale Creek forest service road at 35.9 kilometers. At 36.0 pull off to the right. There are two ways to get down since the road takes a long circular loop down to the site and emerges back on the Harrison West road 200 meters ahead of where you sit pondering.

If you happen to miss this road, the next major marker is the Harrison Lookout Trail sign at 37.0 kilometers. This is a short spur road in an open slash area on the right side. Turn around and head back from here.

The *best* road is the one you are staring at. It is the first one past the Hale Creek bridge. It cuts along the power line then drops down and under steeply to emerge in a logged off slash area. At the end of the slash area (about 1.6 kilometers) there are a few places to pull off and turn around if you have decided to use a truck. The last dive down the hill to the site is steep, with a loose, sandy-gravely surface. No problem going down but coming up is different if you do not have a 4X4 or decent traction. At 2 kilometers, the road curves down opening onto the large flat gravel bay area at the site.

The road cuts across the open gravel area and disappears into the trees, climbing its way (3.5 kilometers) back up to the main road. This section is not the preferred route since there are several creeks that use the road as their pathway, having pushed much of the gravel off to make it feel like a real creek bed with waterfalls. A high clearance 4X4 is essential if you feel it necessary to explore.

If you decide to hike down, this is a perfect loop road of 5.5 kilometers.

SITE DESCRIPTION The site is situated on a small cove guarded by a small rock bluff to the north and by Hale Creek at the south. Between these two is a curved bay with a sand beach and a large open flat gravel camping-parking area. The shoreline is gentle and easily accessed, allowing a canoe or small boat to be plopped into the water.

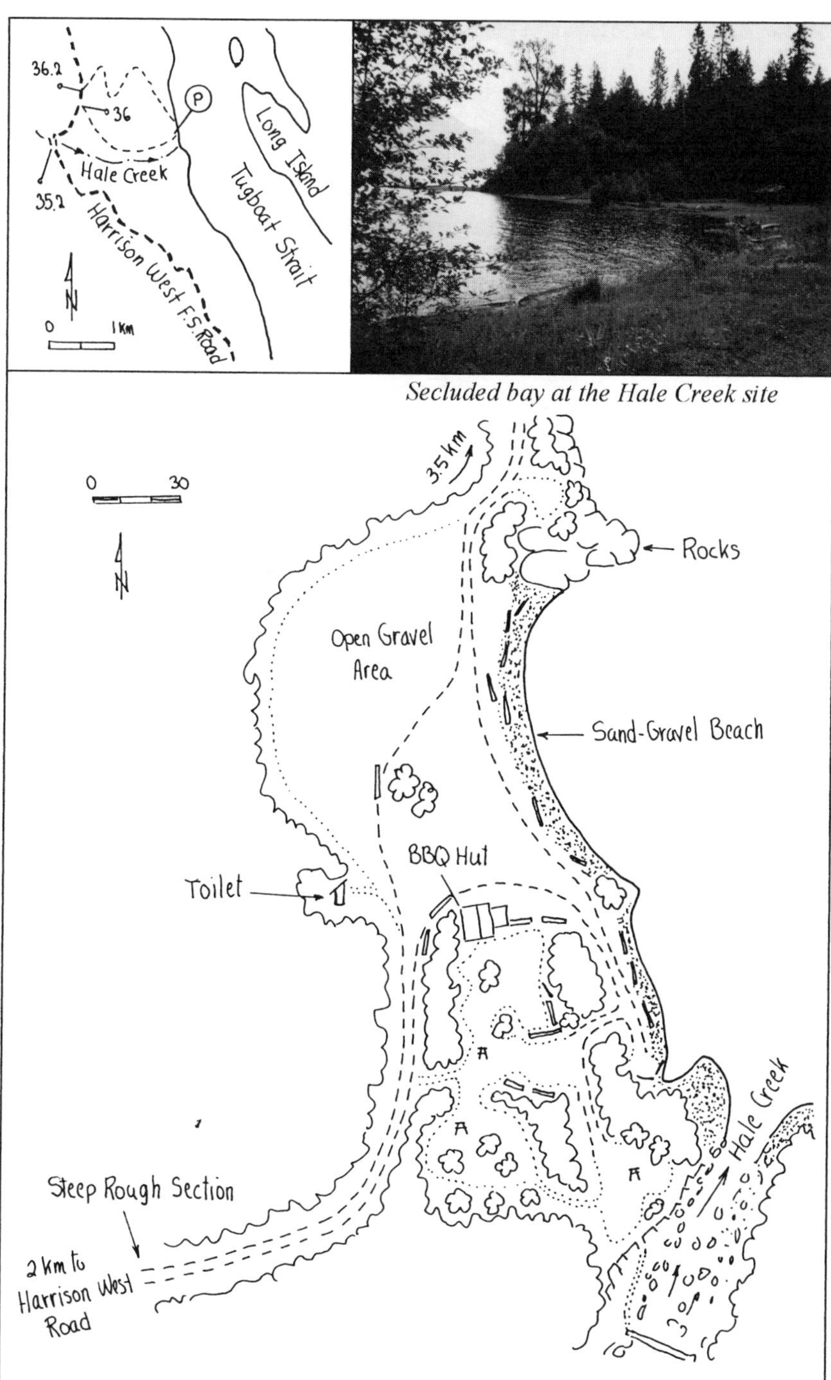

Secluded bay at the Hale Creek site

At the south end of the main clearing there is a unique BBQ hut with a picnic table under a covered porch. In the hut you find a large elevated barbecue ventilated by a smoke hood poking through the roof. In behind are three very large cleared areas set elegantly beneath the tall cedars, each with a picnic table, fire pit and private parking area. The far one along Hale Creek is a most pleasant site completely secluded, with a rather quaint table made out of a stump. Dual fire rings are a feature as is access to the creek which flanks the pad. These are the choice pads but there is also room for open camping in the middle gravel area. The lone toilet, set back in the trees behind the open gravel area services the site.

Another lone but fantastic site can be found at the north exit. It is a secluded open pad large enough for one vehicle, set on the rocks above the water. Tall trees surround the pad making it a very private spot. The site is not large and it is not designed for heavy traffic. As a side note, in summer, when the lake water has dropped, the beach area is much more extensive than that shown in the picture. This opens up beach camp spots for those prefering to be closer to the water.

SPECIAL FEATURES and ATTRACTIONS In addition to the fact that this site is on the beautiful Harrison Lake and you have access to one of its secret coves, the bonus attraction is the nice sandy beach and the unique BBQ hut. This combines to present a special attraction to a few small families. The place is a little paradise, particularly if you are able to come here off-weekends or away from peak season. The gentle shoreline allows one to drop a small boat in easily and this is the closest distance to Long Island Bay, another magic BCFS site on Long Island (see Long Island Bay, site 17). The small islands that guard the entrance to the long picturesque bay can be seen in the distance, about a kilometer away from the site. On a calm day you can paddle across to explore this incredible water world.

SUNRISE LAKE 16

- ☑ CANOEING
- ☑ FISHING
- ☑ MEDIUM SITE
- ☑ TENT CAMPING
- ☑ BOAT LAUNCH

Nestled quietly on a small plateau overlooking Harrison Lake, Sunrise Lake glistens and sparkles with little sign of civilization to disturb its waters. It is a vegetation rich lake making it a perfect habitat for fish. The BCFS site which sits on its shores has to be one of the more perfect spots to be at when the sun rises early morning... probably how it got its name. Although only a kilometer off the main forestry road, the site is truly isolated and it is not easy to get to, requiring a climb up a rough road into this hidden valley. The main attractions are the camping away from the crowds and the fishing offered by the lake. You will need a 4X4 to appreciate it, however.

Glistening waters of Sunrise Lake

FINDING the SITE To get to Sunrise Lake you can use your car if you plan to hike the last kilometer up the hill. Otherwise you need a 4X4 to get you onto the plateau. From Highway 7 at Harrison Mills, pass the Sasquatch Inn (heading east) and turn north, then northwest to take the Morris Valley Road all the way to the Harrison West forest service road. It starts just past the intersection at 11.3 kilometers (past the Weaver Creek salmon hatchery). The Harrison West forest service road is a good all-season gravel road. You will drive 36.7 kilometers in total before you get to the small hidden road to Sunrise. The road is not easy to spot so you definitely want to use your odometer. The spur road cuts back up the mountain at exactly 36.7 kilometers from Highway 7. Your first major warning will come when you hit the Hale Creek bridge at 35.2 kilometers then take a sharp turn right to encounter the Hale Creek forest service road at 35.9 kilometers (it should be marked). Just past this, at 36.7, you will see the Sunrise Lake access road that cuts back up the hill inconspicuously in the bush. You can take this road a short .1 kilometer to reach the power-line, then the rest will depend on your vehicle and how adventurous you are. The road has a continuous steep grade for almost a kilometer with some rough spots where the creek has washed off some of the gravel. There is a particularly rough spot at the crest where you drive on smooth rock outcrop so you need good clearance and traction to spare your vehicle from harm.

At the intersection, the road levels out and the left branch takes you to the swampy side of the lake. This is where there have been some attempts at developing some facilities but these are almost all but swallowed up by encroaching vegetation. The right side takes you to the more popular spot where the open rock outcrop area supports choice campsites, worn open by tires and firewood seekers. This is the best area for water access, launching a small boat, camping and shore fishing.

SITE DESCRIPTION There are two small BCFS recreation sites, one on either side of the lake. The south side was the original focus with three picnic tables, an access road to the lake which served as a launch area and a biffy along the southwest shore. The problem here is that it is about 100 meters to the lakeshore which is marshy, muddy and difficult to access. Even the little lake access road (obviously the old boat launch) is a bit muddy and all but consumed by growth. Farther on, the road ends at a dead end where a lonesome picnic table sits. This is a bit above the lake where the creek enters. You may find a rough footpath leading to the creek and the lake. This area is a bit grown-in and not as popular as the east side.

On the east side, the road curves around to the left taking you almost all the way to the north end before it comes back along the rock outcrop area that overlooks the lake. The main campsite area is at the end of the road. You will pass the lone biffy and eventually curve around into this fantastic open spot where there are several great campsites set nicely on the rock outcrop. Much different, and certainly more appealing than the other side, this is the more popular area.

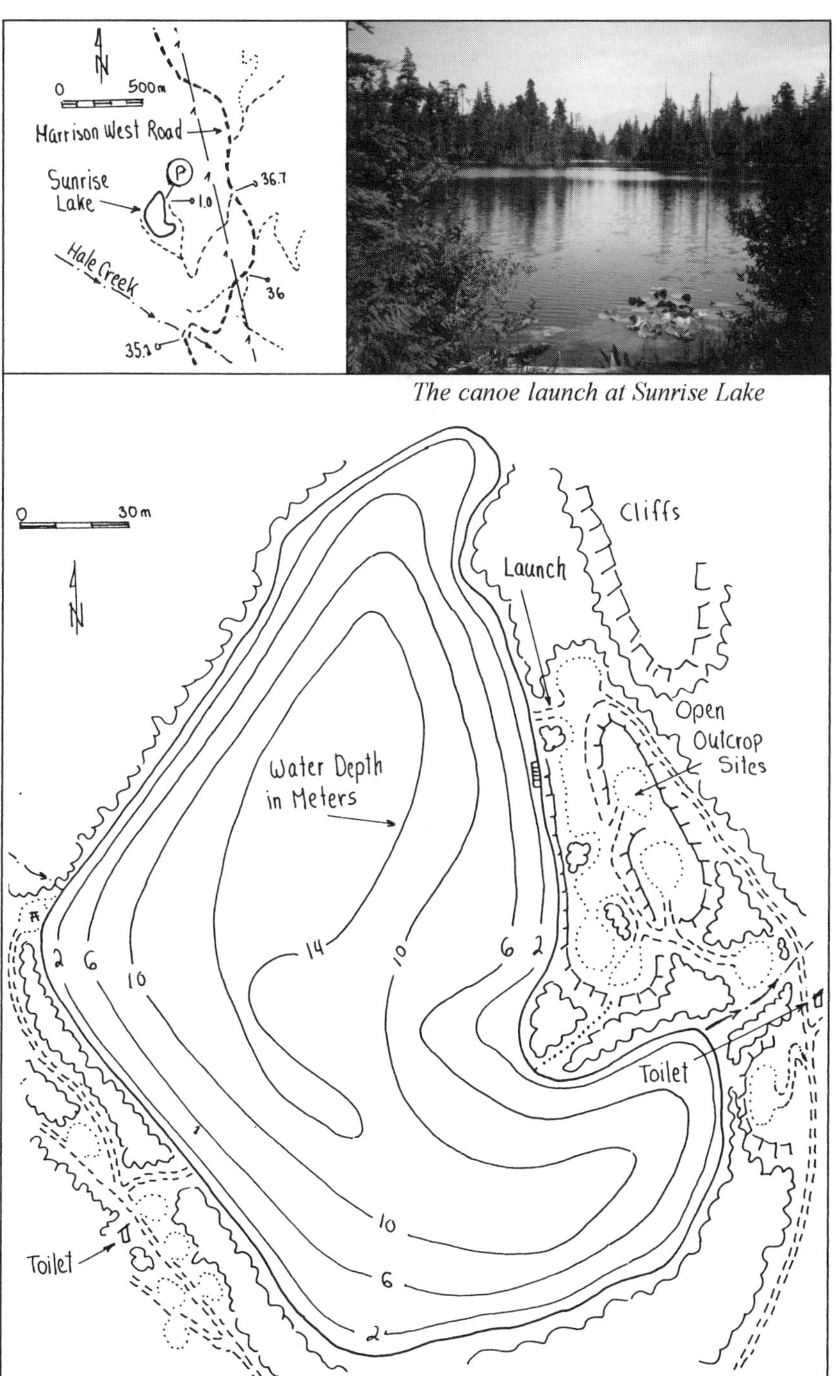

The canoe launch at Sunrise Lake

This area is essentially all open, a majestic little spot overlooking the lake. As you come around the loop by the first site, a short ramp drops to a muddy spot at shore where you can launch a small boat. There is a biffy back at the intersection but why it is set back away from the site is a mystery. Another site is found by cutting down and behind the main rock to a secluded spot by the exit creek. There is also a small wharf below the cliff where the water is deep enough for a dive.

SPECIAL FEATURES and ATTRACTIONS Sunrise Lake is the main attraction here. It is another lake that presents a rather pleasant surprise when you finally get a first look at it. It sits at an elevation of 396 meters, neatly hidden away in a plateau above Harrison Lake. At five hectares it is a decent-sized body of water tucked between rock outcrop and heavy forest. Unlike its close neighbor Wood Lake, this lake requires a short 4X4 jaunt or hike from the main forest service road. As short as it is, the road is just difficult enough to keep the mass of eager campers away. They end up staying at Wood Lake and Twenty Mile Creek so it is one of those quiet, secret, pristine places definitely worth a visit. If you want to give your 4X4 a quick workout and drive up here, make sure you take a canoe. If you are hiking in, take a bellyboat. You won't regret the effort. You will find this an excellent place to camp, canoe and fish.

Fishing The lake has an excellent shoreline for fishing, particularly on the east side where the water drops quickly to six meters off the rocks. This makes it an easy cast into the water, right from your camp fire if you happen to get the prime spot. The lake has rainbows in it but no stocking program is in effect, probably because it doesn't need it. In fact, the whole shoreline drops quickly to ten meters, especially near the west elbow where the stream enters. With the exception of the rocky outcrop area on the east shore, the rest is lined with marsh, debris and brush, not good for shore fishing. A good possibility for trolling or fly fishing is where the stream enters on the west elbow. You can access it from the end of the road where the isolated campsite, table and rough trail can be found. The lake water depth drops rapidly here.

Canoeing If you can drive up here make sure you bring a canoe. This is a magic place to explore. The lake has a varied shoreline with marsh, coves and rocks and is well-protected from the wind. The lake deepens to a maximum of 14 meters in the center, allowing a deeper troll just above the vegetation level. No power boats are allowed on the lake plus it is nicely protected and not too large, so a paddle or electric motor is very appropriate.

LONG ISLAND BAY 17

☑ BEACH
☑ BOATING
☑ BOAT HARBOR
☑ TENT CAMPING
☑ SWIMMING
☑ SMALL SITE

This BCFS site has a special attraction since it is accessed by boat only and it sits in one of the most protected, picturesque bays of Harrison Lake. The setting is as much of a reminder of the ocean coast as you can get. Long Island Bay is a long thin channel on the west side of Long Island, an 8 kilometer thrust of forest covered rock in the middle of Harrison Lake. This bay is as pretty as you can find, offering an impressive place to set anchor and play in an emerald green, watery paradise especially designed for the aquatic recluse. Almost completely protected from wind and waves, this bay makes a very refreshing stop for any one with a boat.

The incredible "unofficial" camping site inside Long Island Bay

FINDING the SITE It is safe to say, given the size of Harrison Lake, and its sometimes hostile wind and waves, that this bay is best visited by a good sized boat. There are two formal places to launch a cruiser, one at Harrison Hot Springs and one at Green Point. The most logical is Harrison Hot Springs since it can accommodate any sized vessel. Once launched, point the boat north and head 20 kilometers to the tip of Long Island. The bay is about half way up the west side of the Island, guarded by Deer Island.

But for those who dare the odd adventure in smaller boats, it is possible to get a small boat in at Ten Mile Creek, about five kilometers south of the bay or at Twenty Mile Bay, about 5 kilometers north of the bay. It is also possible that the forestry has blocked Ten Mile off to prevent congestion, but is worth a try. Directions to Ten Mile follow, while directions to Twenty Mile are in the site following this one. From the Twenty mile site it is possible to paddle across to the northern tip of Long Island then paddle down along the inside shoreline to the bay.

To launch at Ten Mile Creek you need to drive 29 kilometers from Harrison Mills along the Harrison West forest service road. This marks a short spur road that takes you .9 kilometers down a spur road where you will find a picturesque bay at lakeside (turn right off the Harrison West road, then turn left at .7 kilometers for a short drop to lakeshore). There is a small gravel opening at the end of the road big enough for only a few cars or campers. Although not an official boat launch, this little bay and easy shoreline are kind enough to let you launch a small boat and kicker. From here you head along the shore north past the tip of Long Island to the bay.

There is another fantastic alternative if your only vessel is a canoe or a small boat. The hitch is that you need a 4X4 to get down to the BCFS Hale Creek site (15). *Make sure the canoe is strapped on... and don't think about a trailer unless it is <u>small</u> and you have a 4X4.* From the beach it is a mere 1 kilometer of paddling to the mouth of the bay and on a calm day this is indeed a magic trip. To get to Hale, check out the directions under the Hale Creek site.

SITE DESCRIPTION The site sits at the south end of the long narrow secluded bay, completely protected on all sides. Several small islands guard its entrance, while the inside shorelines are mostly forested, offering a thin strip of rocks, and a smattering of sand-gravel spots. A rather distracting feature is the set of private cabins that line the inside north shore opposite the BCFS site. The south shore is not populated. At the end, twin docks (one for the Harrison yacht club) and the other belonging to the BCFS provide easy landing to the main public site. On shore at the site, there is a small grassy spot, backed by forest then rock cliffs. The docks lead to a small open area to pitch a tent. The feature attraction is the barbecue shack set back in the woods, making it an excellent place to have a group picnic.

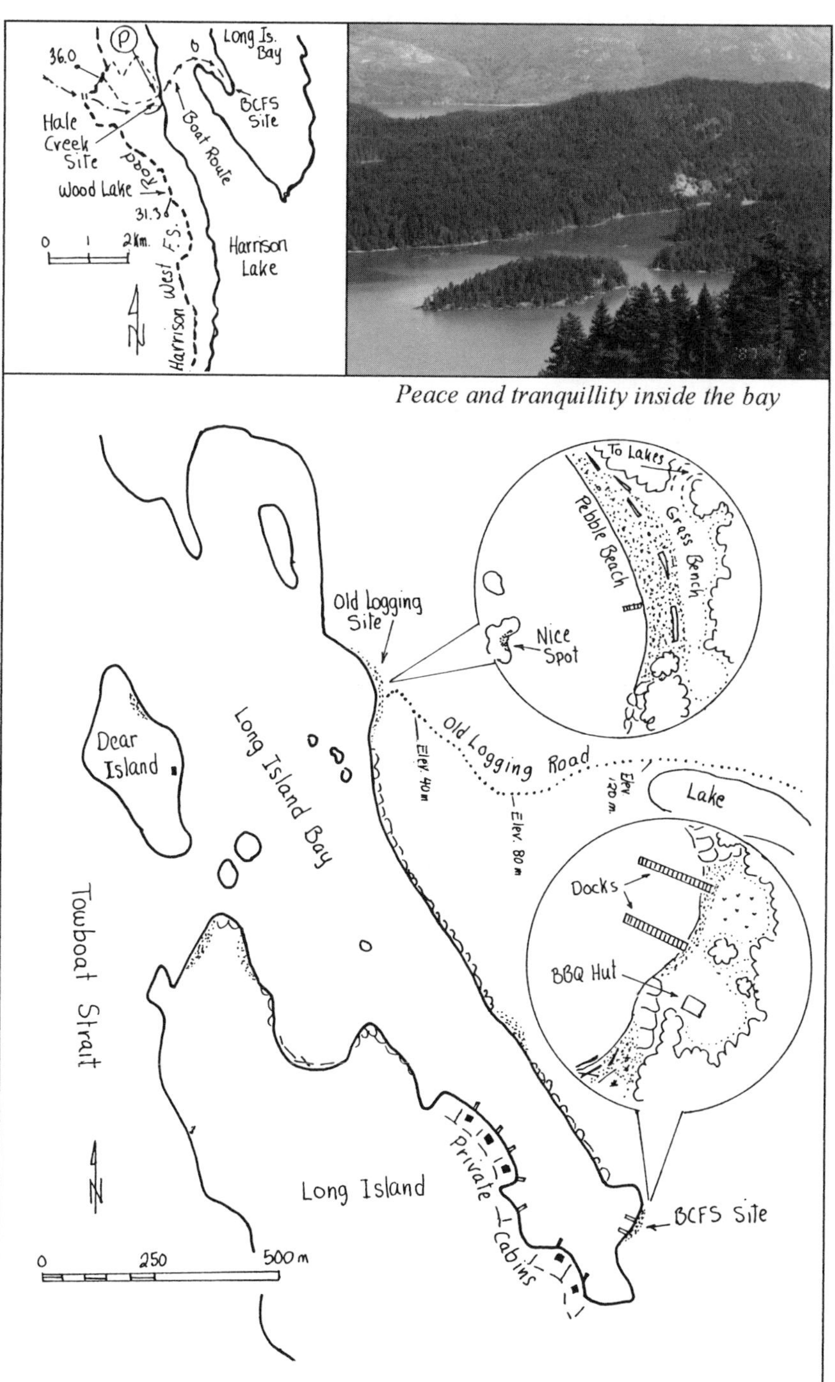

Peace and tranquillity inside the bay

SPECIAL FEATURES and ATTRACTIONS Harrison Lake, being the largest fresh water lake in the Fraser Valley, accounting for a staggering 21,780 hectares of open water can become as hostile as it is beautiful. Long Island Bay is one of those places that is so protected it is almost an oddity. Once you enter the bay, a whole new world appears. The placid emerald green waters lap the little island shores, creating a picture of peace and serenity.

Perhaps the best feature of the bay is the south inside shore and the little islands that guard the entrance. On the shore there is a cove with a fantastic stretch of gravel beach, fronting a grassed bench before this gives way to the pine trees. The area used to be part of a logging operation, most signs now adsorbed into wilderness, but this presents a most fantastic site to camp and sun... there is even a small makeshift dock to help beach a larger vessel. But on the shore there is a wide secluded grassy bench perfect for several campsites. Just opposite this site is a small chain of rocky islands, one with a miniature beach and a few shady trees. This is an absolutely magic spot resembling the Gulf Islands.

Another aspect is the island itself which is 8 kilometers long, reaching several hundred meters high. The relatively flat ridge along the center has several good sized lakes strung along it. An old logging road cuts across the island to the other side to Scherrer Bay, starting on the shore at this old logging site. It is now only a footpath on the overgrown road bed but still distinguishable. There are three good sized lakes on the top, the first being a mere 1 kilometer hike and about 20 minutes from the beach. The trail passes close to two while a branch wanders of to the third called Comet Lake.

TWENTY MILE CREEK 18

- ☑ BEACH
- ☑ CANOEING
- ☑ BOARD SAILING
- ☑ FISHING
- ☑ BOAT LAUNCH
- ☑ BOATING
- ☑ KAYAKING
- ☑ TENT CAMPING
- ☑ SWIMMING
- ☑ RECREATION VEHICLES
- ☑ TRAIL BIKING
- ☑ LARGE SITE

This site has to be the premier BCFS site in the valley. When we first drove into this place it was totally isolated. After driving through the dark foreboding access road that tunnels through dense trees, this place suddenly opened up to present an enchanted forest... huge Douglas firs against a backdrop of sparkling blue waters. The wind was blowing firmly, swinging the giant timbers gracefully, pushing small white caps onto the pebbled shore. The roar of the wind and the waves, the incredible freshness of the air and the unbelievable setting painted a scene in my memory that I will never forget. When I caught myself and looked closer to see the lakeside setting of the camping pads I really wished that we had come to camp. You will not forget this spot. Just try to choose off season or off weekends because many others have also found this magic place.

The expansive pebble beach at Twenty Mile Bay

FINDING the SITE Take the Morris Valley Road off the forestry access road just past the Sasquatch Inn at Harrison Mills (traveling east). Just as you turn left onto the gravel, zero out and instantly pavement appears pointing the way to Hemlock Valley. Take a right onto the Morris Valley Road and follow it through the beautiful valley for 11.3 kilometers. It is here that the road becomes the Harrison West forest service road. From here you will begin to cut over to Harrison Lake and climb above it once you hit the 18-kilometer mark. To get to Twenty Mile follow the Harrison West Road for 41.5 kilometers where you may want to turn left onto the Mystery Road. Don't. You will end up where the Sasquatch roam. Watch your odometer and continue carefully because things get tricky here. All the maps I have seen are wrong in this area so if you have not been here before, follow these directions carefully.

Continue to 44.7 kilometers to hit a four-way intersection which you go through. The left goes into the hills, the sharp right goes to the logging site. At 45.9 kilometers you will cross Twenty Mile Creek (the creek not the site) and, at 46.2 kilometers, take the right fork. At 46.5 kilometers you should hit a straight stretch, then the BCFS marker will appear on the left. Turn left. If you go straight down to lakeshore you will see the south bay of the recreation site. It is possible to get beach access here and launch a small boat. Take this left spur road which gets a bit rougher and keep right. You will reach the impressive BCFS site at 47.7 kilometers. The road is typically good gravel all the way with the exception of the last 1.5 kilometers. It can get muddy and rough from the 4X4 traffic after a rain.

SITE DESCRIPTION If this is your first trip to Twenty Mile Creek, just drive around the loop through the recreation site. The land projects into the lake, creating coves on either side with crescent beaches made of small stones washed clean by the clear blue lake water. Rock outcrop is interspersed with beach logs and the whole point is forested in tall, swaying timbers. The lack of any underbrush beneath the trees creates a magic park-like setting hard to beat for camping. Most of the campsites are large and distributed between the access road and beneath tall timbers, tucked nicely against the shoreline to give all residents beach property. These are large sites, some with tables and fire pits, all very clean and impressive. Round pebble beach, sunning rocks, shade trees, crystal clean water, logs to nap against... all the best beach attractions are right beside your camping pad. The area is only about two hectares in size containing about 25 large campsites so, on long weekends, you may find it very congested. The area is endowed with several toilets and garbage cans distributed along the central common area. The most likely place to launch a boat is on the open gravel area on the south beach where the road ends up in the lake. Many of the campsites snuggle against the shore, making it easy to launch a small boat.

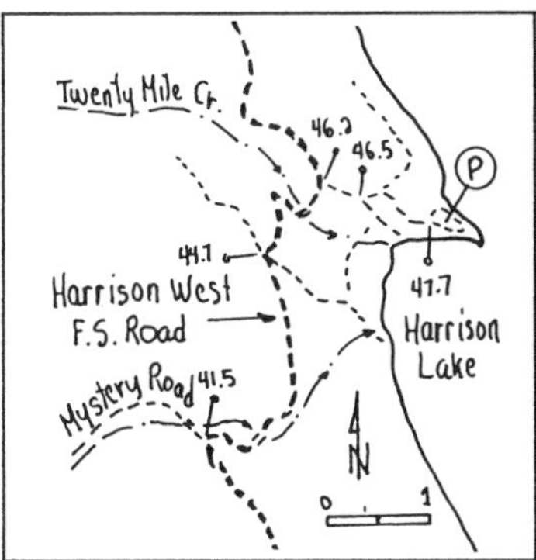

The gravel beach at Twenty Mile Bay

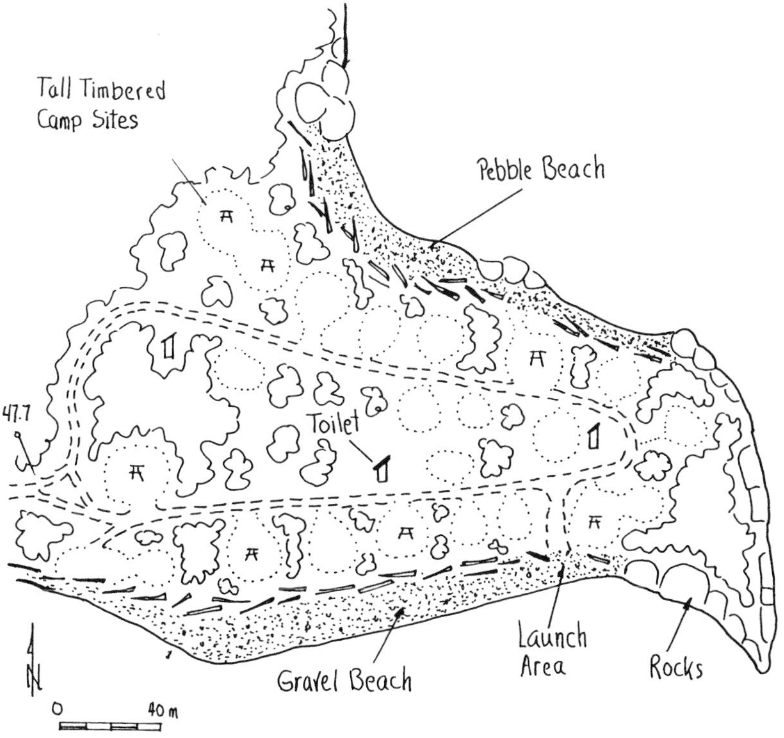

Tall Timbered
Camp Sites

Pebble Beach

47.7

Toilet

Launch
Area

Rocks

Gravel Beach

0 40 m

Timbermens Cove

The point sticks out to the east so there are beaches on either side, the calm one downside of the prevailing wind. The north cove is the prettiest being somewhat protected unless the wind is blowing from the north.

SPECIAL FEATURES and ATTRACTIONS Harrison Lake is the largest in the Fraser Valley, accounting for a staggering 21,780 hectares of open water. It is indeed a spectacular body of water, reaching into remote wilderness areas essentially inaccessible except by boat. The lake is 55 kilometers long with no highways and, despite its impressive size, has relatively few access points. The only real developed part is at the southern tip at the Harrison Hot Springs resort area. So finding access to the lake is a rare treat. For anyone wishing to explore this vast area, Twenty Mile offers a fantastic base camp about half way up. The Harrison West road is the main 'highway' here, actually taking you to the tip of the lake and beyond but, for the most part, this is very remote wilderness. It has only opened up within the last decade, thanks to the conditioning of the logging roads. Due to the steep mountainous terrain and high precipitation, the multitudes of streams have carved deep gorges all the way down to the lake and, as a result, there are very few good access points. Of these Twenty Mile is one of the best.

Boating and fishing If you want to fish in this lake, note that it is deep with the contours dropping quickly to 200 meters. It is also subject to fierce winds and waves so be cautious about open-water boating. Stay close to shore unless you know the lake and you have a big boat. If you need to launch a large boat this is not the place to do it. You need to go to Harrison Hot Springs or Green Point at the south end where there are two good concrete facilities. In this area, it is best to fish where the streams enter along the shoreline especially south of the point between the main shore and the island. Twenty Mile site is directly across from Long Island with its own magic shoreline of beaches, coves, rock shoreline and picturesque places. On a calm day it is easy to paddle across and explore in this area. Of special note is Long Island Bay, a boat only BCFS site covered earlier.

Board sailing. If you can catch a windy day at this place, and there are many, the waves can get quite high and the bay is a perfect place to haul out the board to check out your balance. The wind can get serious, blowing consistently for several hours at a time. This is a rather unique feature of the area. If it gets too rough switch over to the other side of the point.

Trail biking If you want to explore with your 4X4 or a dirt-bike this is a perfect place to do it. The roads (old and new) are everywhere, taking you into every nook and cranny imaginable. The roads into Mystery Valley and past Twenty Mile Creek are particularly suited to exploration. There are hundreds of kilometers of roads in this area.

RAINBOW FALLS 19

☑ BEACH	☑ TENT CAMPING
☑ CANOEING	☑ SWIMMING
☑ FISHING	☑ VIEWING (FALLS)
☑ BOATING	☑ SMALL SITE

The unique feature of this site is the fact that it is accessible by boat only, yet it is only 600 meters away from the main road. The attraction is the spectacular falls that thunder down the cliffs to the east shores of the majestic Harrison Lake. A special spot created by a projection of boulders and sand pushed outwards into the lake by the force of Slollicum Creek, this place is the only flat land along this cliff laden shoreline. The result has been to create a unique gravel-sand beach area, back-dropped by sheer cliffs. If you choose a calm summer day you can paddle a canoe along a spectacular 6 kilometer section of the lake, stopping at this super secluded place to camp, fish, swim or picnic.

Cascade Bay, a secluded fresh water paradise

FINDING the SITE Just before you hit the end of Highway 9 at Harrison Hot Springs, turn right on Lillooet Avenue and drive through the residential area. The road will turn left at the foot of the mountain becoming Rockwell

Road. Parallel the lakeshore for 6.1 kilometers, then turn left to Green Point Park. This is the closest spot from where you would launch your boat. Green Point is a day-use park with good public facilities (also closed for winter). It is the best spot for launching a mid-sized boat (5 to 10 meters). As you enter the park you will see the 'U'-shaped boat launch to the left when you cross the bridge. This boat launch has a well-designed double-concrete pad that offers you the best public facility on the lake plus a large paved parking lot off to the right. Plop the boat in here and park over in the parking lot. It is 6 kilometers along the shore from here to the site. When you start out you will be directly opposite Echo Island. If you have a small boat you should hug the shore to keep away from the harsh winds. You will pass half way as you approach the point of Cascade Peninsula and the lonely little Island call Lone Tree Island... guess why? As you cruise, or paddle along the rocky shores of the lake, and marvel at the escarpments, you will eventually approach a round protruding gravel bar created by Slollicum Creek. It will be seen rushing its battled waters into the lake after crashing down the escarpment. You will hear the roar of the falls even though they are set back in the miniature canyon.

SITE DESCRIPTION This unique place consists of a 200 meter wide circular gravel bar protrusion into the lake, with another circular backdrop of canyon wall at the rear, covering the other 180 degrees. This creates an odd circular shaped piece of flat land... a little paradise. The falls, created by Slollicum Creek, are set back at the south end of the gravel bar. The site has an old landing, a cobble-sand beach, a biffy and some special camping sites. Skirting the beach there is a small forested area, some of which is subject to flooding from high water so it is semi-swampy, covered with scrub trees. Nevertheless, there are a few places to camp close to shore, the main camping area being closer to the falls, set back from the shore. The major attraction is the spectacular falls that thunder vertically down the steep rock cliffs before tumbling into the deep crystal pools. The back of this "U" shaped cove of rock rises quickly and vertically to prevent escape, and provide total privacy from the rear. It also offers tree cover, shade and good protection from winds for camping. At the lakeshore you will find a beautiful gravel-pebble beach. An excellent fishing hole is found at the mouth of the creek.

This site is one of a kind in that it is accessible *only* by boat. Although you can find Slollicum Creek crossing the main road a mere 600 meters away from the falls, it is 360 meters of almost vertical climb to get there.

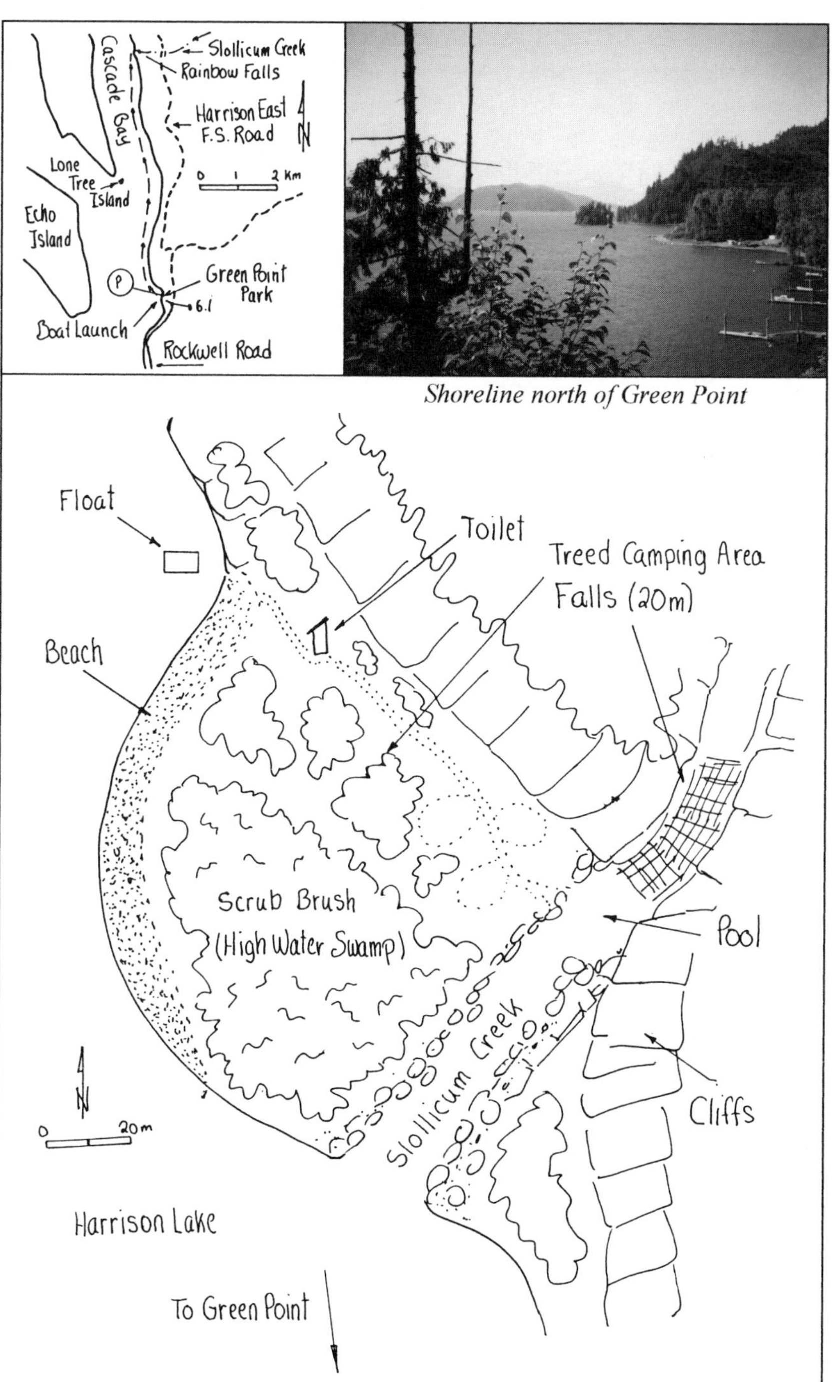

Shoreline north of Green Point

SPECIAL FEATURES and ATTRACTIONS Harrison Lake is the largest in the Fraser Valley, accounting for 21,780 hectares of area. It is indeed a spectacular body of water, reaching far into remote wilderness areas essentially inaccessible except by boat. The lake, 55 kilometers long, has no highways, only logging roads along much of its perimeter. The easiest access and most developed part is at the southern tip at Harrison Hot Springs. This east side of the lake has been opened up by the main logging road following the shoreline sometimes several hundred meters above the water. Due to the steep, mountainous terrain there are very few access points along the lake despite its size. In many cases the drop to the lake is vertical for several hundred meters. This particular site is an excellent example of the many secret coves and beaches on the lake.

Rainbow Falls is situated in a very protected bay called Cascade Bay. It is possible to see the bay from a lofty position on the Harrison East road. If you have a small boat and feel up to it, you can paddle up into the head of Cascade Bay, an incredibly beautiful, protected section of the lake and marvel at some of the summer cabins.

CASCADE PENINSULA 20

☑ BEACH
☑ CANOEING
☑ FISHING
☑ BOATING
☑ TENT CAMPING
☑ SWIMMING
☑ TRAIL BIKING
☑ SMALL SITE

The unique aspect of this site is that it is so pretty a setting it became too popular and, at the time of writing, the access road was closed to vehicular traffic. Situated on the shores of Harrison Lake, on a quaint pair of little bays called Cooks and Macs coves, the site features emerald green waters, secluded bays with pebble beaches, and a rocky shoreline resembling an ocean shore. This is an exceptionally nice place, well worth a visit even if you have to hike down for the day. It is now reserved for boat traffic but the site can still be enjoyed by hiking in.

Secluded pebble beach at Cascade's Macs Cove

FINDING the SITE There are two basic choices here. You either take a boat from the nearest launch at Green Point or you drive along the Harrison East forest service road to the closed road and walk 1.6 kilometers down the hill to the site. Let us first get there by boat.

Just before you hit the end of the Highway 9 at Harrison Hot Springs, turn right on Lillooet Avenue and drive through the residential area. The road will turn left at the foot of the mountain to parallel the lake, becoming Rockwell Road. At 6.1 kilometers you hit the turnoff to Green Point where you launch your boat. Green Point is a day-use park with good public facilities. It is the best spot for launching a mid-sized boat of 5 to 10 meters. As you enter the park you will see the 'U'-shaped road to the boat launch on the left when you cross the bridge. This boat launch is a well-designed double-concrete pad that offers you the best public facility on the lake. A large paved parking lot is off to the right.

Plop the boat in here and park in the parking lot. It is about 12 kilometers along the shore from here to the site. When you start out you will be directly opposite Echo Island. If you have a small boat you should hug the shore away from the harsh winds. As you approach the point of Cascade Peninsula and the lonely little Island called Lone Tree Island you need to cruise to the outside of it since Cascade Bay is a dead end. From here you hug the shore all the way around to the top of the peninsula where you will encounter two small coves. These twin coves, Macs and Cooks, mark your destination, each lined with arched pebble beaches.

By car you would follow on past the Green Point turnoff and at 7.3 kilometers drive straight through onto the Harrison East forest service road, rising above Harrison Lake. At 18.9 kilometers, pull off the road as you encounter the spur road on the left. This road dives down to Cooks Cove and Cascade Peninsula but it is blocked off and closed. Pack up and start your short hike of 1.6 kilometers to the bay. The grade is steep, dropping consistently all the way down to the bay.

SITE DESCRIPTION The site sits right in the face of the south winds that can blow fiercely down the lake but the coves are reasonably protected. Situated on the shore, the site has an alternating mix of pebble beaches, and rocky buttresses that project out into the water. There are actually three little bays here, each lined with a protected shoreline of pebble beach before it gives way to the dense bush. Between the coves is a large projection of rock and each cove has a smaller short projection of flat rock perfect for sunning and diving off into the clear cool waters.

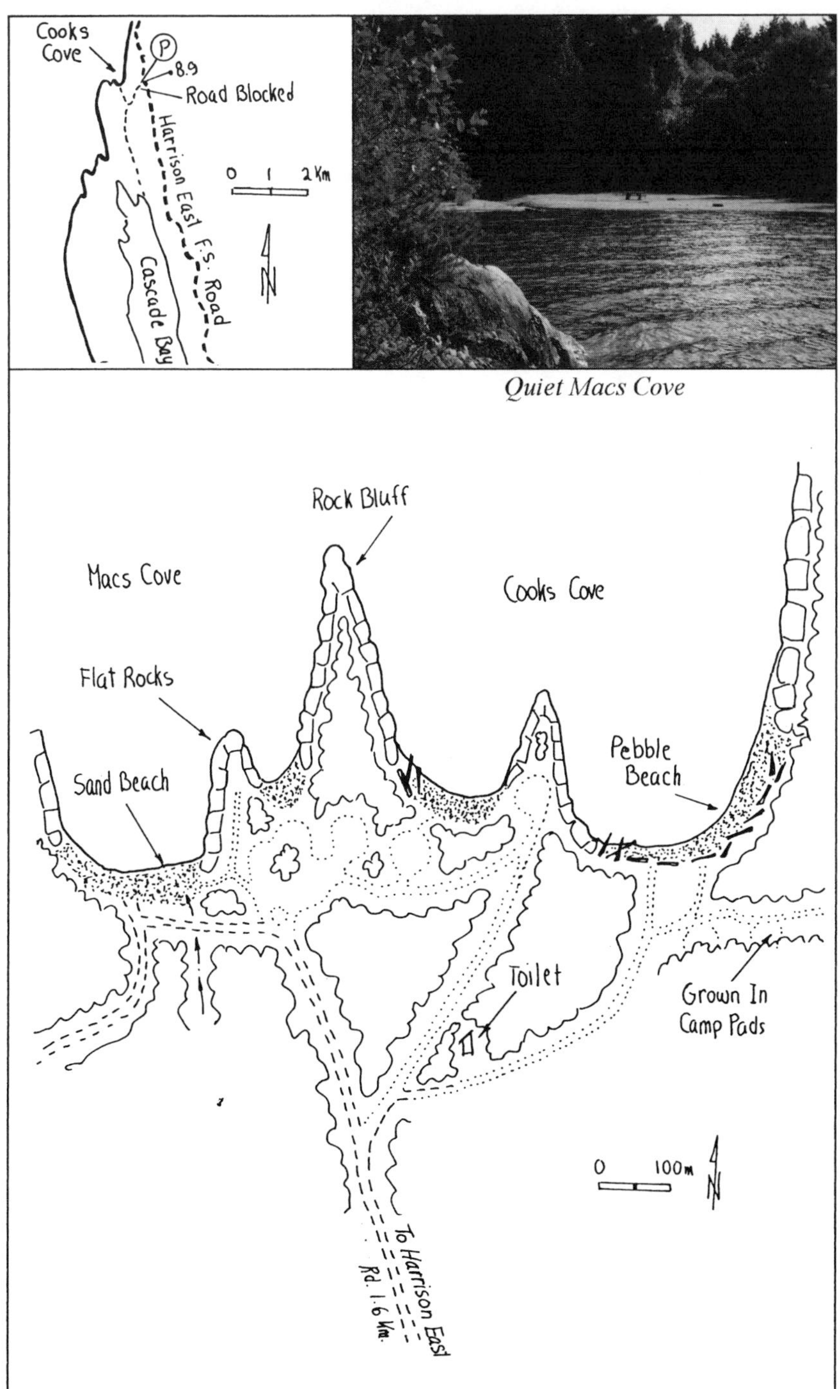

Quiet Macs Cove

On shore, the flat land alternates between groves of deciduous trees and small open meadows creating one of those picture-perfect spots that we all dream about. The camping pads are set along the shoreline offering fantastic settings under the shade trees. There are not many pads here but those that exist are beauties. There is also a biffy centrally located. Other than this, mother nature has paid some special attention to this place, carving out a memorable mixture of pleasing scenery.

BEAR CREEK 21

- ☑ BEACH
- ☑ CANOEING
- ☑ FISHING
- ☑ TENT CAMPING
- ☑ SWIMMING
- ☑ LARGE SITE CLOSED

Once not so long ago this large gravel projection into Harrison Lake had to be the most active camping spot on this side of the lake. It probably was one of the nicest places so close to the access road... and it actually still is but, as the story goes, hooligans and un-appreciating cads abused the place making it a den of mischief. So the forestry placed a huge ditch across the access road and closed the site... a real pity. It is easy to see why the place was popular. Bear Creek is seen as the backdrop thundering down the escarpment then rolling through the gravel bar on the south side. An emerald green cove with a sand beach borders the north. And in the middle stand gigantic cottonwoods and conifers shading at least 40 unbelievable camping pads. A gravel beach in front of it accents it all. But it is still officially closed. I include it here because there is a chance that the new forestry policing program will work well enough that they re-open it soon. In the meantime you can still day-use the site.

Park-like setting of Bear Creek

FINDING the SITE Just before you hit the end of Highway 9 at Harrison Hot Springs, turn right on Lillooet Avenue and drive through the residential area. The road will turn left at the foot of the mountain to parallel the lake, becoming Rockwell Road. At 6.1 kilometers you pass the turnoff to Green Point and enter Sasquatch Park. At 7.3 kilometers, drive straight through onto the Harrison East forest service road, rising above Harrison Lake. Continue driving until 22 kilometers, thus crossing over the Bear Creek bridge. You should notice a large flat gravel shoreline, heavily wooded, in a park like setting on the left. There is little place to park here except for the narrow shoulder and a wider spot on the left of the road just at the bend 100 meters ahead.

SITE DESCRIPTION From the Harrison East forest service road, a short access path drops down along the creek bank to the lower forest but a large ditch blocks traffic. If you walk down the short path which used to be the road, onto the flat area you will emerge into a very pleasant open wooded area which still has signs of many (at least 40) camping pads, all fantastic cleared locations under large trees. The whole area widens like a large fan as it slopes gradually to the gravel beach. Bear Creek tumbles over huge boulders into the lake on the left, forming a choice fishing spot at the mouth. The right side opens out into a pebble-sand beach cove, guarded by a craggy rock buttress. The area is large and, with the exception of the gravel beach, completely covered with giant poplars and firs. There is no thick underbrush except for the occasional bush, strategically left alone by the dominant trees just to say they care. A magic spot this is, but no facilities.

SPECIAL FEATURES and ATTRACTIONS Without a doubt, this place is a rare attraction. The east side of the lake does not have too many car accessible places except for Cogburn (next site) that flank the road and at the same time allow easy access to the water. Most of the east shoreline drops vertically to the water, sometimes several hundred meters from above. It is well worth the effort to stop and walk into the place... maybe even for a swim in the cove... or cast a line into the water for a big dolly. Oh, by the way, if you have a look across the road where Bear Creek decides to leave the mountain you will note a most spectacular waterfall thundering down the cliff, and I mean thundering! There is a short footpath to the bottom pool.

On a philosophical note. In some ways I suppose that closing the site will at least protect the area so that a few can appreciate it. It is hard to question the forestry in their protective tactics in this regard. But it would be nice to see more of us appreciative people have an opportunity to enjoy a night out in such a magic place. The new forestry program of "checking in" on sites is designed to discourage the rowdy and encourage the more appreciative people. It is actually working, slowly chasing out the bad by bringing in more of the good.

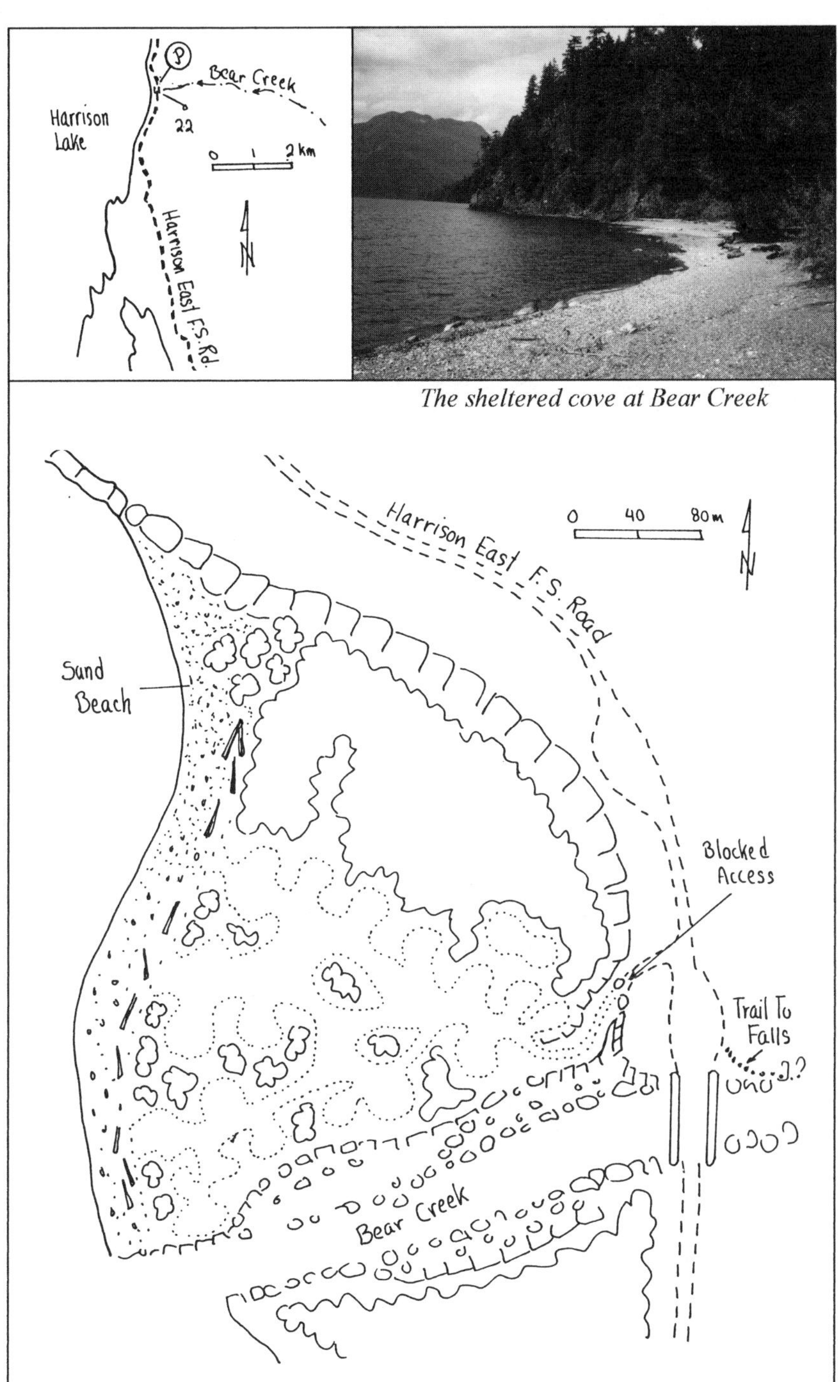

The sheltered cove at Bear Creek

COGBURN BEACH 22

☑ BEACH
☑ FISHING
☑ RECREATION VEHICLES
☑ CANOEING
☑ TENT CAMPING
☑ SWIMMING
☑ MEDIUM SITE

Harrison Lake makes one big bend from north to northwest at about its midpoint where Cogburn Creek meets the lake at a place called Bear Creek logging camp. Just north of here at the mouth of Silver River, is a bit of a peninsula that acts as a buttress deflecting those harsh winds from the north. Along the shore just south of Bear Creek Camp is a long strip of protected sand and pebbly beach, called Cogburn Beach that extends several kilometers. Along this stretch is a narrow strip of land that drops down to lake level offering easy access to the shore. At the south end of this is an incredibly beautiful spot nestled in the tall timbers overlooking a sheltered and peaceful pebble beach cove. Not surprising, this place has become a BCFS site.

The view north from Cogburn Beach

FINDING the SITE Just before you hit the end of Highway 9 at Harrison Hot Springs, turn right on Lillooet Avenue. Drive through the residential area.

The road will turn left at the foot of the mountain to parallel the lake, becoming Rockwell Road. At 6.1 kilometers turn right passing the road to Green Point. As you enter Sasquatch Park, the road changes to good gravel still suitable for a car. At 7.3 kilometers drive straight through onto the Harrison East forest service road, rising above Harrison Lake. The next section rises above the lake to give excellent views of its magnificent expanse. It is not until you cross Bear Creek at 22 kilometers that you come back down to the elevation of the lake, to swiftly climb up again. Finally, at 27.1 kilometers, and a solid share of dust, you will see two small parking areas on the left, the second one marking the Cogburn Beach site.

SITE DESCRIPTION This is another one of those rare, magic places bordering a pebble beach on this side of the lake that are easily accessible. Situated right beside the main road, the site stretches along the beach, spread out through the tall trees. In this particular section, the land slopes gradually from the road to the shore, offering less than 10 camping pads. These are set strategically under large trees clear of underbrush on either side of a small creek that runs through the area into the lake. The two small parking areas service the camping pads on either side of the creek. There are several picnic tables, garbage cans and a biffy. Note that the biffy is at the north part since there are more pads in that area. The beach stretches for the full length, within a few meters of the camping pads. From the parking lots it is reasonably easy to carry a *small* boat or canoe to the shore, even though there is no formal launch facility. If you need to get closer with a small trailer you can drive another kilometer to where the road gets much closer to the beach. There are a few spots where it is possible to drive down onto the pebble beach. Remember, however, that this shore is *not* a formal launch.

SPECIAL FEATURES and ATTRACTIONS Harrison Lake is of course the largest body of fresh water in the Fraser Valley, accounting for 21,780 hectares. With the exception of the southeast private shoreline around Harrison Hot Springs, its eastern shoreline is inaccessible except by boat. There are only a few areas you can drive to and get access. The stretch at Cogburn is a particularly long expanse that is readily accessible making this area a special treat. From here it is possible to explore this unique area either by small boat if you stay close to shore or on foot if you are a land lubber. There are also many roads reaching deep into the valleys and up into the mountains in this area. Exploring and dirt biking are natural attractions in this type of terrain but be advised that this area is being actively logged. Cogburn Beach is therefore an excellent place for a base camp to explore from.

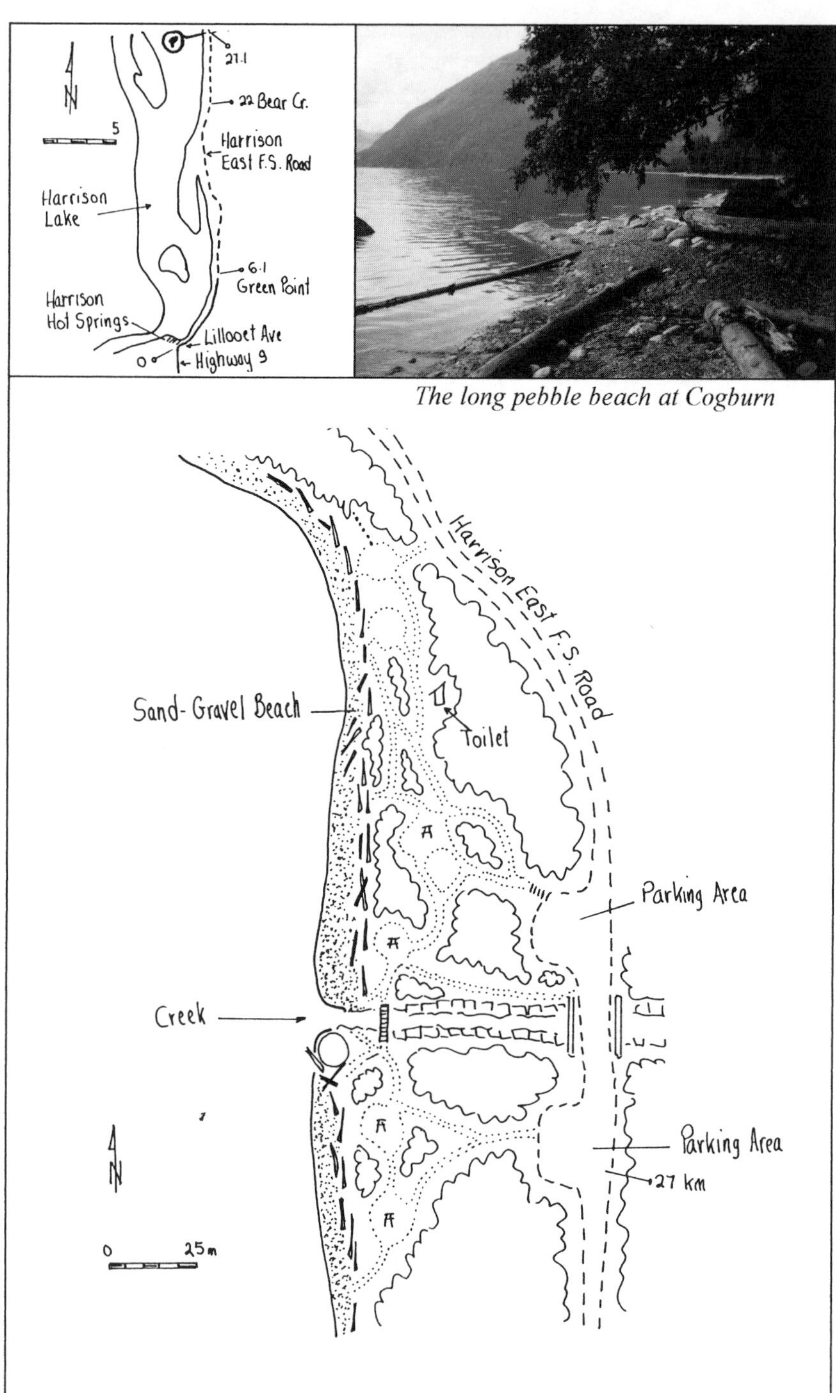

The long pebble beach at Cogburn

TAMIHI CREEK 23

- ☑ FISHING
- ☑ WHITE WATER
- ☑ TRAIL BIKING
- ☑ LARGE SITE
- ☑ KAYAKING
- ☑ TENT CAMPING
- ☑ RECREATION VEHICLES

It is very difficult to understand what kind of site this used to be. When you first approach it you will think you have entered an old trailer park of some sort. If you drive into the back of the site, you find a unique BCFS site with its usual rustic pads and facilities. Situated at a rather turbulent bend in the Chilliwack River where Tamihi Creek joins it, this flat grassed area skirts pools which provide excellent fishing and downstream from a rapid run which provides a professional kayak run. A set of concrete strips demarcate all the key areas, pads, roads and parking, all defined by these strips of cement that are designed to keep order... a particularly odd concept for a BCFS site. Nevertheless the parking pads are adjacent to a grass camping area making absolutely perfect spots for good sized recreational vehicles to park. But if you prefer the usual BCFS pads, head to the back!

Peaceful camping along the Chilliwack River at Tamihi

FINDING the SITE Take the Chilliwack Lake Road from the Vedder Road 9.9 kilometers east up the Chilliwack Valley. Just as you cross the river and note the hanging kayak markers on the left up-river section of rapids, get ready to turn right onto the Tamihi forest service road. A short .4 kilometers back down the river on the other side takes you across Tamihi Creek and to the entrance of the site.

SITE DESCRIPTION The site sits on a wide flat bench, partially grassed up front and partially bushed in deciduous trees in the back. The front section was probably a trailer park at one time, containing a perimeter road making a long ellipsoidal loop enclosing a nice grassy area. In contrast to this, the back section follows the usual BCFS philosophy of dirt road, bush and biffy, and natural pads.

The front or east section where you first enter has a series of formal gravel parking pads demarcated by cement dividers. These are well placed at strategic angles around the perimeter road making it easy to park a trailer and camper. They all have access to a grassy open area where you have fire rings, picnic tables and even the odd bench. Most popular, of course, are the grass sites along the river bank where you can hear the roar of the river in background stereo to complement your crackling camp fire. A short meter drop down gets you o the rapids in this area. There are about 10 places available surrounding the central area where you have an open play field, some tall poplar trees for shade plus several central picnic tables and garbage cans. The biffy is set back by the entrance.

The west, or back section is a bit different, offering a series of alternating camp pads set nicely in the trees. Quite a contrast to the "up scale" facilities to the east, there are approximately 20 sites distributed in the woods around the continuation of the loop road. These are much more rustic and less formal than their eastern counterparts. The north and west section is within close proximity of the river. There is a lonesome central biffy to service this section.... well used I'm sure.

SPECIAL FEATURES and ATTRACTIONS A very unique attraction found here is due to the nature of the river in this section. Just north of the main bridge over the Chilliwack River is a section of water that tumbles fiercely over and between huge boulders. Since this part drops rapidly in elevation, the water gushes and pauses in back eddies in an alternating sequence to form a perfect gauntlet for those brave enough to maneuver their crafts through the rapids. The unique run has become so popular that cross wires have been strung over the river in strategic places.

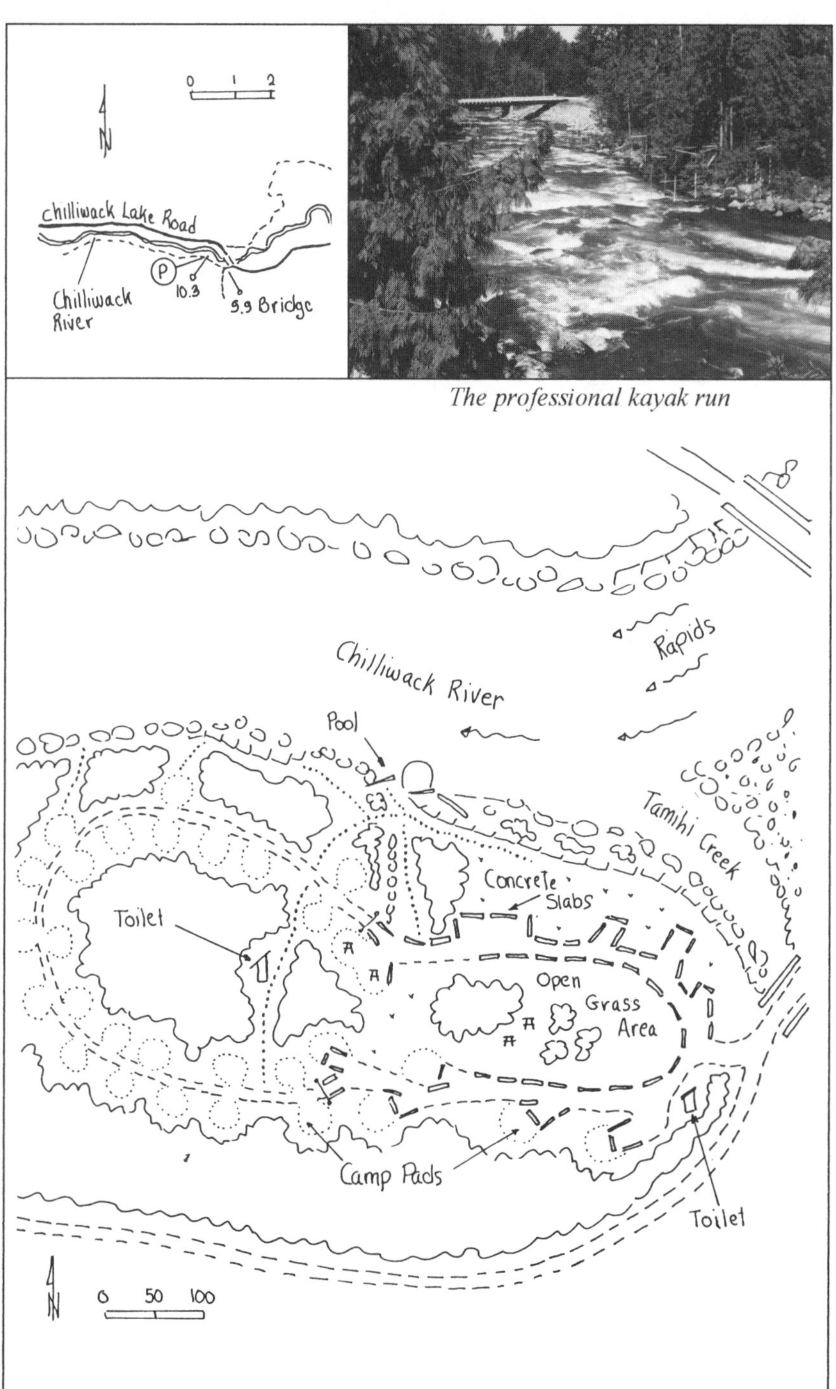

The professional kayak run

These vertical markers hang down just above the water. Kayakers can therefore maneuver their boats, in true competition style, to further their skills.

Fishing Still another neat treat offered by the river is the Steelhead, salmon, and trout fishing that has given this river international fame. The river is fast moving, dropping rapidly to form large green pools and endless runs alternating from fast moving white water to flat runs where the water slows... perfect spots to see large Steelhead or salmon resting momentarily to strike anything that passes. In season, the river is literally dotted with fishermen spread 10 meters apart in just about every available open gravel bar on the river. At the site, the river comes surging down toward the campsites to be forced into a turn. The pools thus formed are deep and inviting to a fisherman.

Trail biking South of the site is an extensive network of logging roads reaching well up the Tamihi Creek valley. The Tamihi-Chilliwack forest service road also forms a web of old roads to the west of the site. While this main road parallels the south side of the river, numerous spur roads reach high up into the mountains. For a trail biker this extensive system offers endless places to explore. Many of these are un-maintained so a word of caution is in order. There is nothing to beat the feeling of wind in the face and the power of that bike reflected by the 50 meter dust rooster tail... except for a fallen tree, big rock in the road or an unexpected washout. Somehow picking gravel out of your broken teeth has a tendency to change the type of excitement rapidly!

ALLISON POOL 24

- ☑ FISHING
- ☑ WHITE WATER
- ☑ RECREATION VEHICLES
- ☑ KAYAKING
- ☑ TENT CAMPING
- ☑ MEDIUM SITE

Anybody who is in the know about Steelhead hotspots has heard of Allison Pool. This fantastic run of water is formed by two snake-back turns in the Chilliwack River as it alternates between rock walls and gravel bars, surging down a run, then slipping smoothly through deep pools. The recreation site skirts this section of the river stretching along the wooded shoreline between the river and the road, giving excellent access to one of the more famous pools on the river. Totally open on the campsite side, the deep pools, gravel-sand bars and rushing green waters along this stretch offer one of the most easily accessed, and actively fished sections of the Chilliwack River.

A world famous fishing pool

FINDING the SITE From the Vedder Road, drive along the Chilliwack Lake Road for 13.5 kilometers. The road is paved, with no obstacles to thwart even your Ferrari. At this point pull off to the left onto a gravel road... carefully if the Ferrari is new. Just as you pull in, a circular parking area will magically appear before you. Park here. The road continues a short distance to the left, then all the way down to the river but it is blocked to traffic.

SITE DESCRIPTION The site stretches in a strip, from the circular parking lot near the main road all the way to the river, over a length of about a kilometer. Centered on this thin strip of heavily wooded forest, is an old road that has the camping pads laid out all the way to river frontage. The main parking lot is small, not designed for more than 5 vehicles. Tall trees offer nice cover for about 10 camp pads usually demarcated by open clearing. A few picnic tables are still in place and two biffys service opposite ends. The south area near the parking lot is more popular since you can drive onto a few pads. To prevent congestion, a set of enormous rocks and a ditch have been placed immediately past the first camp pad to stop vehicle access. If you prefer seclusion, and want water frontage, the sites closer to the lower pool at the bend of the river should be the choice. A 600 meter walk is required thereby making them less popular but certainly more private.

From the central road, several short trails poke through the woods emerging on the large gravel bar, its size being dependent on the season and the amount of water in the river. The bar is quite extensive, offering a wide area to cast a line from. Several sandy pockets are found along the river where people have camped and cooked their prizes.

SPECIAL FEATURES and ATTRACTIONS Needless to say, fishing is the prime activity at this place. In season the deep emerald pools and fast, short white water runs attract hoards of fish and anglers. Both Steelhead and salmon are the targets. But this activity should not overshadow the nature of the camping sites. These are pleasant and functional being adjacent to the large gravel bar, even in off-season. In mid summer, the river settles down creating cool pools connected with runs of white water. For river swimming, or fooling about with a small flotation device, this place excels. You just have to work around the fishing season or you can find yourself being hauled in.

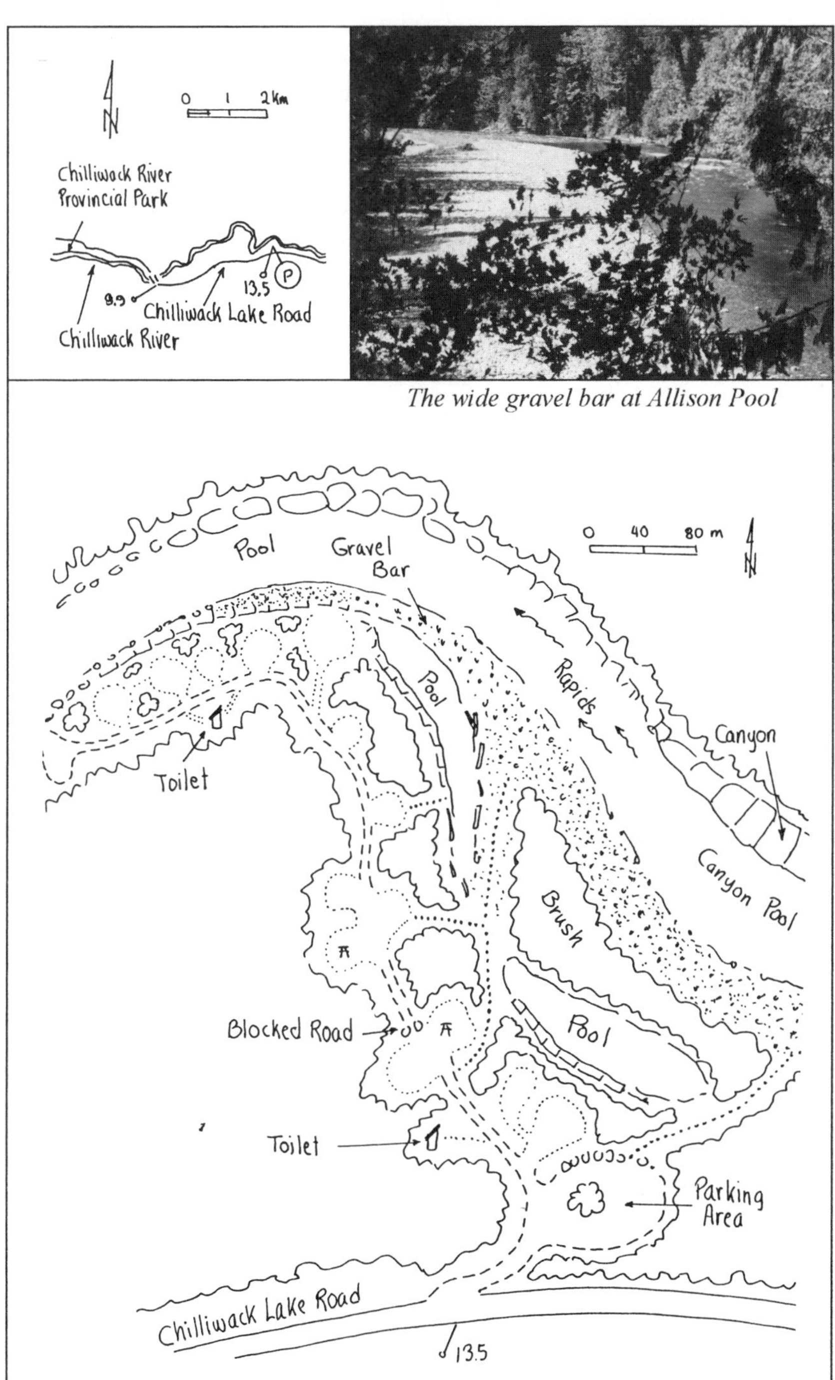

The wide gravel bar at Allison Pool

THURSTON MEADOWS 25

☑ FISHING
☑ HIKING
☑ RUBBER RAFTING
☑ TENT CAMPING
☑ RECREATION VEHICLES
☑ MEDIUM SITE

There are not too many places on the Chilliwack River where you have good access for larger recreation vehicles. The Chilliwack River Provincial Park and the BCFS Tamihi sites are a few. There is another spot, however, where the river takes a snake like bend just before it turns to parallel the main road. The large river bend thereby bounds a nice pleasant, flat, open meadow area adjacent to the road. Central to the area is the large open grassy meadow fringed with trees, called Thurston Meadows. Being open and accessible, it is easy to bring in a larger camper or even a Winnebego if you so prefer and have easy access to the river.

Open grass meadow at Thurston

FINDING the SITE From Vedder Road take the Chilliwack Lake Road 16.7 kilometers east. At this point, a gravel road will appear on the left, along with an open grass meadow. Pull in here and drive around the loop to get a feel for the place. The road will not present any hardships even for a larger trailer since the meadow is open and flat.

SITE DESCRIPTION A pleasant open site, Thurston has been rimmed with several camping pads, some set on the bank of the river, others adjacent to the meadow but set in the shade trees. As you enter the area, the left sites are open and but less attractive even though they are perched on the bank of the river. The sites farther in are more appealing set under a few tall trees on the river bank, a little more picturesque. The northern area at the top of the bend is heavily wooded, also with a few excellent spots skirting a small tributary. A biffy set in the woods services the area. Continuing around the loop, there are fewer pads as the distance to the river increases. These are secluded, offering sanctuary from the heavy crowds that gather here in summer. Central to the whole site is the grass playing field, used to park larger vehicles, play ball, practice casting, or try whatever open meadows entice you to do.

SPECIAL FEATURES and ATTRACTIONS The ability to bring in a large trailer or a camper is a bonus here. The open meadow is also nice in that the kids can play safely while pop tries the new rigging. The area immediately adjacent to this site is not good for fishing primarily because the water is shallow and rock laden forming few runs for the fish to slow down. There are many other excellent spots that can be reached from this place if it is used as a base camp. In summer, rubber rafting is a possibility but the river drops fast through the boulders having little time to form pools. In this particular region there are many other popular runs and pools for fishing. Close by, Pierce Creek Trail offers a very challenging hike and Allison Pool has the fish while Foley Lake offers canoeing. See the description of these areas included elsewhere in this book.

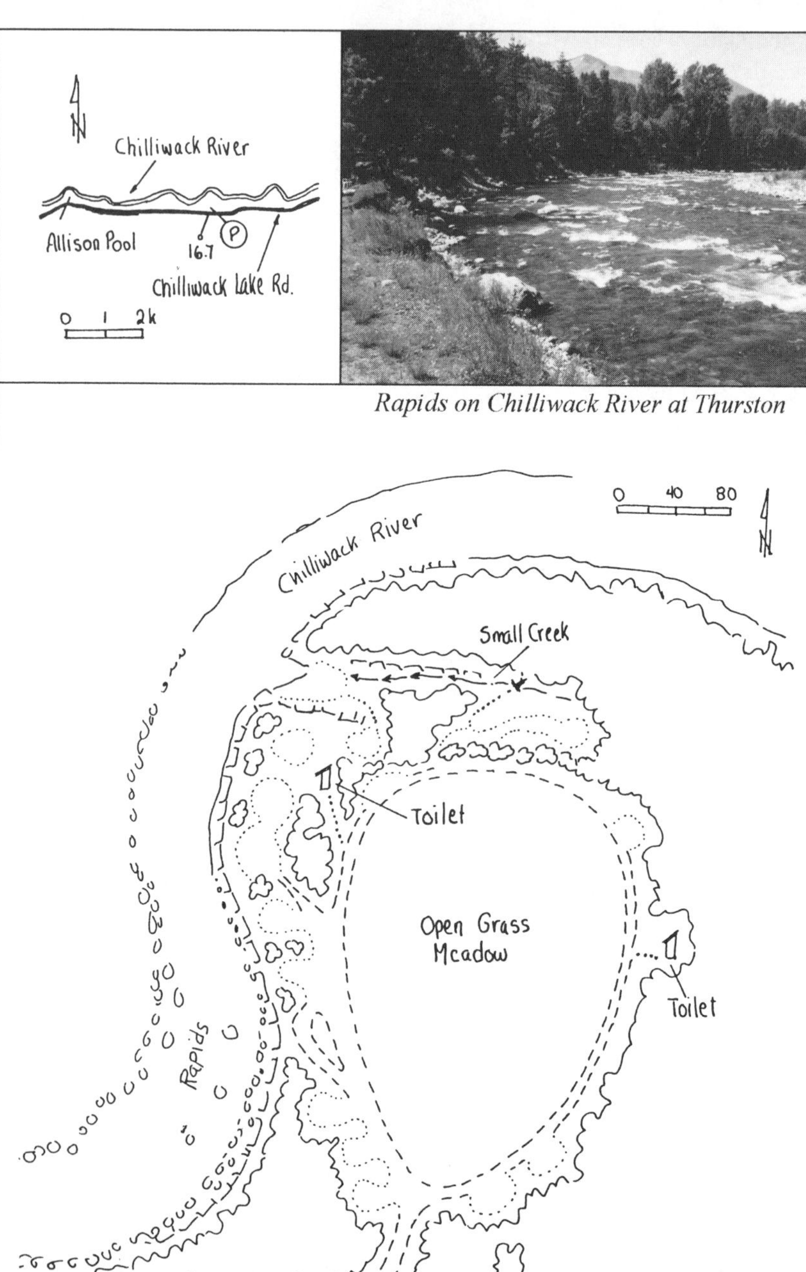

Rapids on Chilliwack River at Thurston

PIERCE CREEK 26

☑ FISHING ☑ TENT CAMPING
☑ HIKING ☑ SMALL SITE

This site is a tough one to describe because it is so small and essentially featureless. Yet is serves as a small parking lot and trailhead for one of the more fantastic, and enduring unofficial trails in the valley. From this site one can take a difficult but rewarding journey up Pierce Creek to Pierce Lake and to the headwaters below the lofty Mount MacFarlane. This trail is not in the BCFS inventory because it is in poor shape, difficult and even dangerous. For this reason, I am including the trail as a feature of the immediate area.

Unbelievable clear, cool waters of Pierce Lake

The hike is a spectacular excursion into the wilderness and the Forestry has started a plan to improve the rough sections. BCFS has indicated that they are also looking to reroute the trail to make it less precarious. This trail will lift you to rare unforgettable alpine lakes and meadows, places where snow dominates the ecosystem for most of the year, past two unbelievable lakes, and a spectacular elevation of 2099 meters.

FINDING the SITE To find the site, you must first find the little access road that cuts south directly off the Chilliwack Lake Road at the 22.2 kilometer mark (from the intersection of Vedder Road and Chilliwack Lake roads). There is a forestry sign on the road but if you blink you will miss it easily. The short access road is sandwiched between two sections of the Mount Thurston Correctional Institution land. This is a short pot-holed gravel road of less than .5 kilometers that terminates at the BCFS site and a small parking area, also the trailhead for the Pierce Lake-Mount MacFarlane Trail.

SITE DESCRIPTION The site is very small, tucked away in a forested section at the foot of the mountain. Offering little more than a few spots to camp at, the open grassy area is not more than 40 meters across. Facilities include the BCFS biffy, a picnic table and a place to park your car. The site serves mostly as a trailhead parking area. At the far end of the site is the trailhead for the Pierce Lake Trail described below.

SPECIAL FEATURES and ATTRACTIONS It is the trail from the site that offers the attraction. The little valley which the trail leads to was once a focal point of the Forest Service that spent some effort originally developing it and the few simple facilities at the trailhead. Since then the trail has deteriorated and the Forest Service actually discourages use because there are some dangerous sections.

Pierce Lake Trail All that said, if you decide to don the boots you will begin the unforgettable adventure at an elevation of 320 meters. From the trailhead the footpath takes you east winding upwards abruptly through the second growth forest dominated by ferns and moss. This continues for about .8 kilometers where it reaches Pierce Creek and an elevation of 400 meters, Now you begin the real ascent paralleling the creek. After getting a few views from some rock slides, you will begin the climb averaging about 100 to 150 meters vertically for each half-kilometer. At two kilometers you will have climbed to 800 meters and at 2.5 kilometers you take a slight dip to cross the creek at elevation 950 meters. From here the trail has deteriorated and is poorly marked so be prepared. This is a *dangerous* section laden with rotten and fallen logs, some originally making up the trail bed. The steep terrain and the drenched meadows make for precarious and slippery sections. The trail eventually rises above the lake which comes into view suddenly, a spectacular dark jade green body of water set down in a basin. A side trail dives down to the right to the lake.

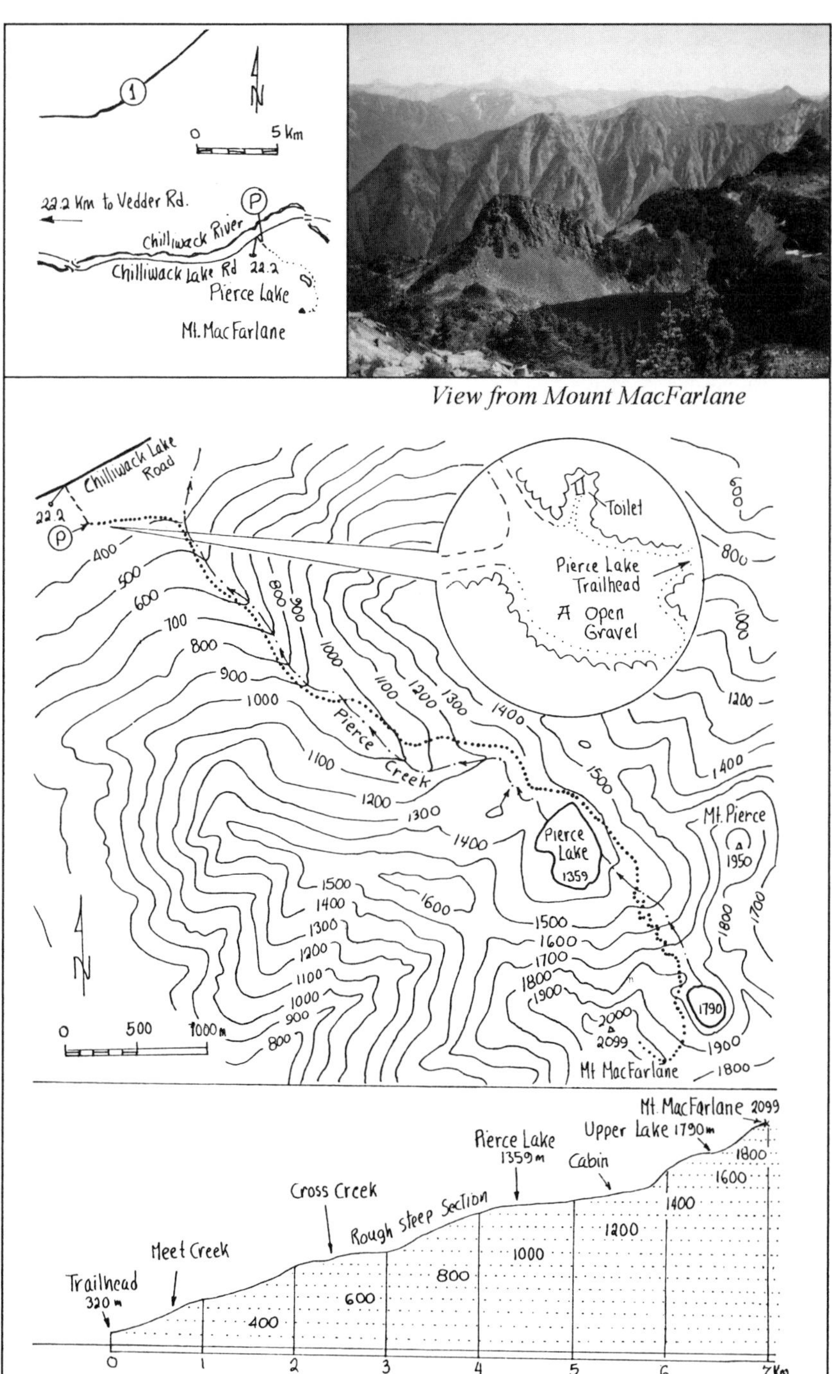

View from Mount MacFarlane

The total distance is 4.3 kilometers taking about 3.2 hours without stops. The elevation is 1400 meters at the north end of the lake.

The trail continues onward to the meadows at the southeast end of Pierce, crosses over by the old cabin site (1440 elevation). From here you cross the creek and follow it rising aggressively up the alpine valley headwall through loose talus to finally emerge in the small alpine meadow just below the second lake (1790 meters). The total distance is about 6 kilometers to the small upper lake, the terrain now mostly bald rock. From here the best approach is from the southwest basin of the lake. In the last 800 meters of horizontal distance, you will climb from elevations of 1800 to 2040 meters into the basin below the ridge. The approach will take you south, then curve southwest to finally emerge on the south end of the peak, 7 kilometers total distance from the car and a staggering elevation of 2099 meters. Note that from the upper lake you can follow the ridge north about a kilometer to reach Mount Pierce. It is only 1950 meters high!

Without a doubt, the trail to the lake is an adventure. The trail climbs deep into alpine and up the bald exposed peaks. At the time of writing the trail was being fixed through the bad section. This alpine vegetation, the almost permanent snow and the unsurpassed scenery are well worth a visit. Note that this trip is *not for the inexperienced* or out-of-shape person. The total return trip is 14 kilometers with an elevation gain of 1779 meters and remember the same elevation drop on the way back is sure to give your knees a reason to ache. The best way to approach this trip is to do it in August and be prepared to stay overnight at Pierce Lake.

Pierce Lake is very high up on the south ridge above the Chilliwack Valley at an elevation of 1350 meters. Set in the valley between Mount Pierce and Mount MacFarlane (2099 meters), the lake is 18 hectares making it a reasonably good-sized body of water. Pierce Lake and its little neighbor farther south form the headwaters of Pierce Creek, draining the valley toward the Chilliwack River. Little is written about the lake and hiking to it requires a considerable effort.

Fishing is another feature of the lake. This is a deep lake reaching 30 meters in the middle with falls at the lower end where Pierce Creek spills over the lip of the lake. All this forms a secret fly fishing lake for those keen enough to endure the hike. The lake is reported to have good-sized rainbows at 30 to 40 centimeters with some cold-water fighters reaching 50 centimeters (that's 20 inches!) and dollys over 30 centimeters are also reported in this lake. Unless you have an Olympic buddy who can pack a belly-boat up here, you will have to fish from shore; probably the reason the lake has not been over-fished. Fisheries have been diligent about stocking the lake quite consistently.

CAMP FOLEY 27

- ☑ FISHING
- ☑ SMALL SITE
- ☑ WHITE WATER
- ☑ KAYAKING
- ☑ TENT CAMPING
- ☑ RECREATION VEHICLES

By no means the largest site in the area, one can hardly say that Camp Foley is subject to crowding. Positioned on a flat wooded section of Chilliwack River as it roars under the bridge, this nicely wooded area is designed to make you and the river one. The river rushes through this section at a good pace tumbling over large boulders creating a constant backdrop of water roar. Not surprising, the forestry lists the feature here as kayaking. In support of this you find much of the site is a parking area from which it is very easy to slip a kayak into these exciting waters.

Prime camping and kayak launch at Camp Foley

FINDING the SITE Take the Chilliwack Lake Road 26.3 kilometers from the intersection of Vedder Road and Chilliwack Lake Road. The road is paved so the old limo is just fine. As you approach 26 kilometers you drive over the bridge across the Chilliwack River. On the left you will see an open gravel area. The short road parallels the main road below the left shoulder. At 26.3 kilometers you need to take a wide turn left onto the Chilliwack-Foley forest service road and turn sharply to backtrack on that little gravel road. The gravel parking lot is just a short way in.

SITE DESCRIPTION Not a lot to boast about in terms of quantity of camping pads, namely three, the site makes up for it by quality. These are well cleared pads right along the river bank, set under the trees in the shade. The little site beside the bridge has a tiny beach. The larger pad at the end of the parking lot is also set nicely in the trees beside the river. The bonus here is the picnic table. A lone biffy and a few garbage cans are the support services. Much of the site is an open gravel area that serves as a parking lot and also extra camping spots for campers or recreation vehicles.

SPECIAL FEATURES and ATTRACTIONS The attraction is the cool tumbling waters of the river that are so easily accessed here. They rush through at quite a pace. If you are into kayaking or river swimming, this is a challenging run. Chilliwack Foley forest service road follows the bank of the river 1.2 kilometers further on making a walk-back or pickup easy if you want to try it. The river is quite rough here, characteristically laden with large boulders, and quick drops providing a gauntlet of white water runs and challenging back eddies all the way down this section of the river. In fact, if you are more courageous, there are three more BCFS sites along this section from Camp Foley that can be used as pick up or as camping points to come down to, depending on your stamina, courage and expertise. These are described in the next sections, but here is the sequence.

From Camp Foley take the Chilliwack-Foley forest service road on the left. At 2.0 kilometers cross the bridge over Foley Creek and make a left turn onto the Chilliwack-Chipmunk Road. Still keeping left at 3.8 kilometers continue straight through ignoring the Chipmunk forest service road and at 4.4 kilometers a road peels off to the left into the Chipmunk Peninsula site (stop 1). Continuing straight through you will have a good look at the canyon rapids and reach the next site, Rapids (site 2, quite appropriately named!) at 7.0 kilometers. If this is not enough to satisfy you, rush on to Eagles Roost at 7.8 (site 3).

Remember, however, that the river is rough. The section after Chipmunk Peninsula surges through a narrow canyon that calls for a look before you leap. The road is placed close to the edge of the canyon here so it is easy to do just that. From here the water changes to a long white run down past the Rapids site. If your destination is Rapids make sure someone is standing there waving because you will whip by like a shot.

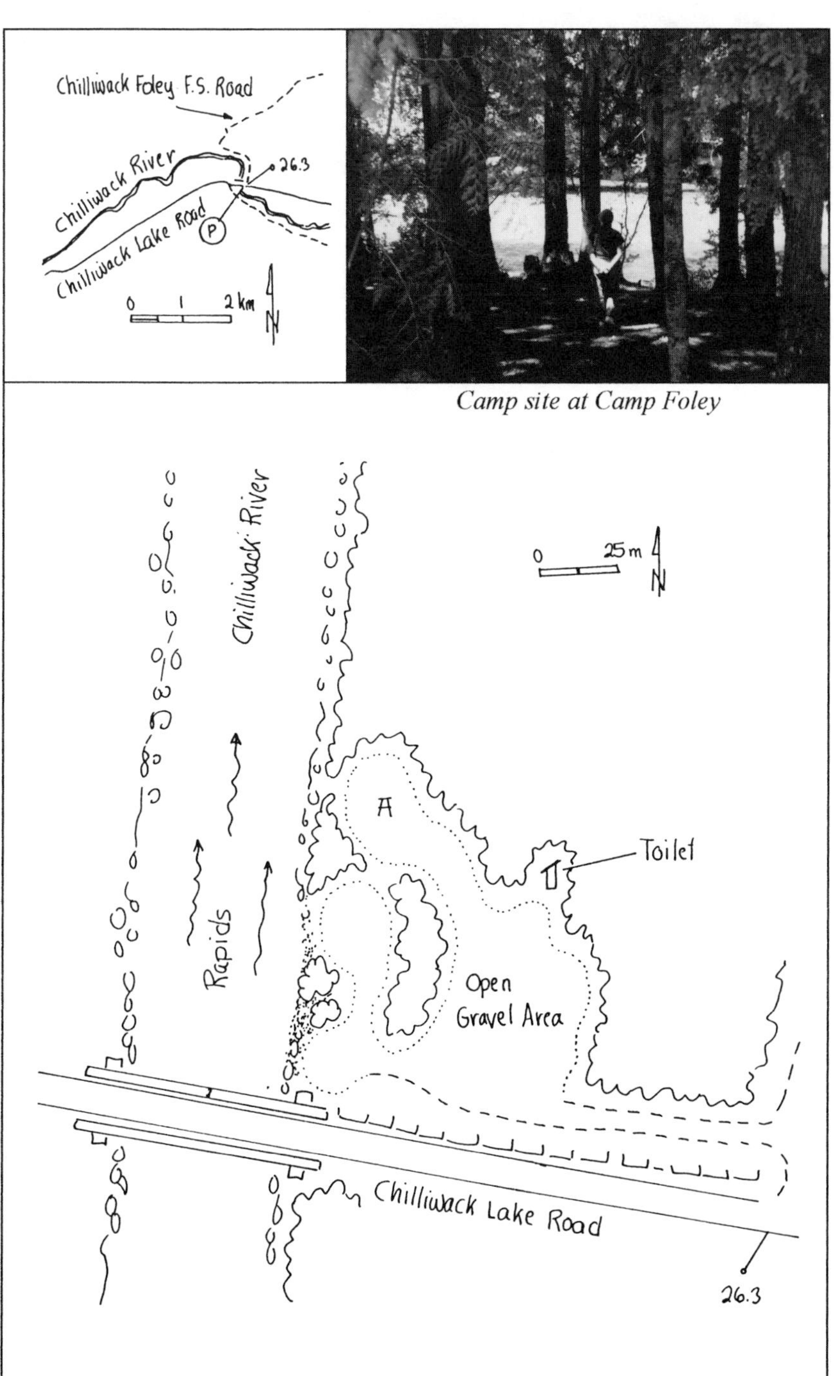

Camp site at Camp Foley

CHIPMUNK PENINSULA 28

☑ TRAIL BIKING
☑ FISHING
☑ WHITE WATER
☑ MEDIUM SITE
☑ KAYAKING
☑ TENT CAMPING
☑ RECREATION VEHICLES

The constant roar of the white waters of Chilliwack River is only part of the noises common to this shady place. The other part comes from the roar of the dirt bikes that the youngsters are allowed to use for buzzing around the campsites. This in itself is a unique feature since there are not too many places that allow this. So junior buzzes through the maze of special trails while Dad runs the rapids and Mom worries... seems a bit one sided. In any case, the Chipmunk peninsula pokes out forcing the river to make a wide swing around this pretty forested setting. Here several nice camping spots have been placed around the river bend where the water is quite swift and white.

The raging rapids at Chipmunk Peninsula

FINDING the SITE Take the Chilliwack Lake Road from the Vedder Road out of Vedder Crossing for 26.3 kilometers. Just as you cross the Chilliwack River you will encounter the Chilliwack-Foley forest service road on the left. Turn left and zero out the odometer. At 2.0 kilometers cross the bridge over Foley Creek and make a turn left on the Chilliwack-Chipmunk Road. At 3.8 kilometers continue straight through ignoring the Chipmunk forest service road. At 4.4 kilometers a road peels off to the left. This is the entrance to the loop road through the site.

SITE DESCRIPTION As you drive down into the dark forested area and keep left to approach the river, the road turns to follow the river and loops back. The first larger pad is situated to the left before the loop, a nice quiet and private site beside the river. From here the pads are distributed along the loop road alternating side to side. There are about 14 pads formally laid out with a central biffy mid-loop. Just opposite the biffy, a trail cuts down through the trees in a magic setting then cuts back along the river to loop back to the main sites. There are several open areas along this stretch where a camp can be set up. The bike trails are on the north side of the road.

SPECIAL FEATURES and ATTRACTIONS

Trail biking Quite an unusual aspect of this site is a trail specially designed for the junior trail bikers. It is reasonably safe to say that usually campers are somewhat irritated by those dastardly buzzing bikes roaring by their campfires, but not here! The people that frequent this site will most likely have a common plight... to teach the little guys the glory of trail biking. To support the idea, a neat short trail has been beaten out in the sand of the peninsula, making a little loop down to the river and around so the really little guys are always within hearing distance. The real bike trails, however, are found on the other side of the road. On this side, away from the campsites, there is an elaborate network of specially designed paths to challenge the new enthusiast. But for the more senior bikers, this particular area is completely networked with logging roads. The Army Bench, Foley, Airplane Ridge, and Chipmunk forest service roads all lead to high elevation labyrinths to explore.

Kayaking The peninsula juts out forcing the river to take a large loop around the camping area. Through this section the Chilliwack River has a fairly narrow channel and drops at a steady grade, creating quite a set of rapids. The water is fast moving and somewhat dangerous but if you are an avid kayaker, you may try this section for a challenge. Before you do, drive down to the next site called Rapids (described next) and note the river as it surges through the canyon. This section of river is not for amateurs, so beware. If you plan to launch up river, see the site called Camp Foley.

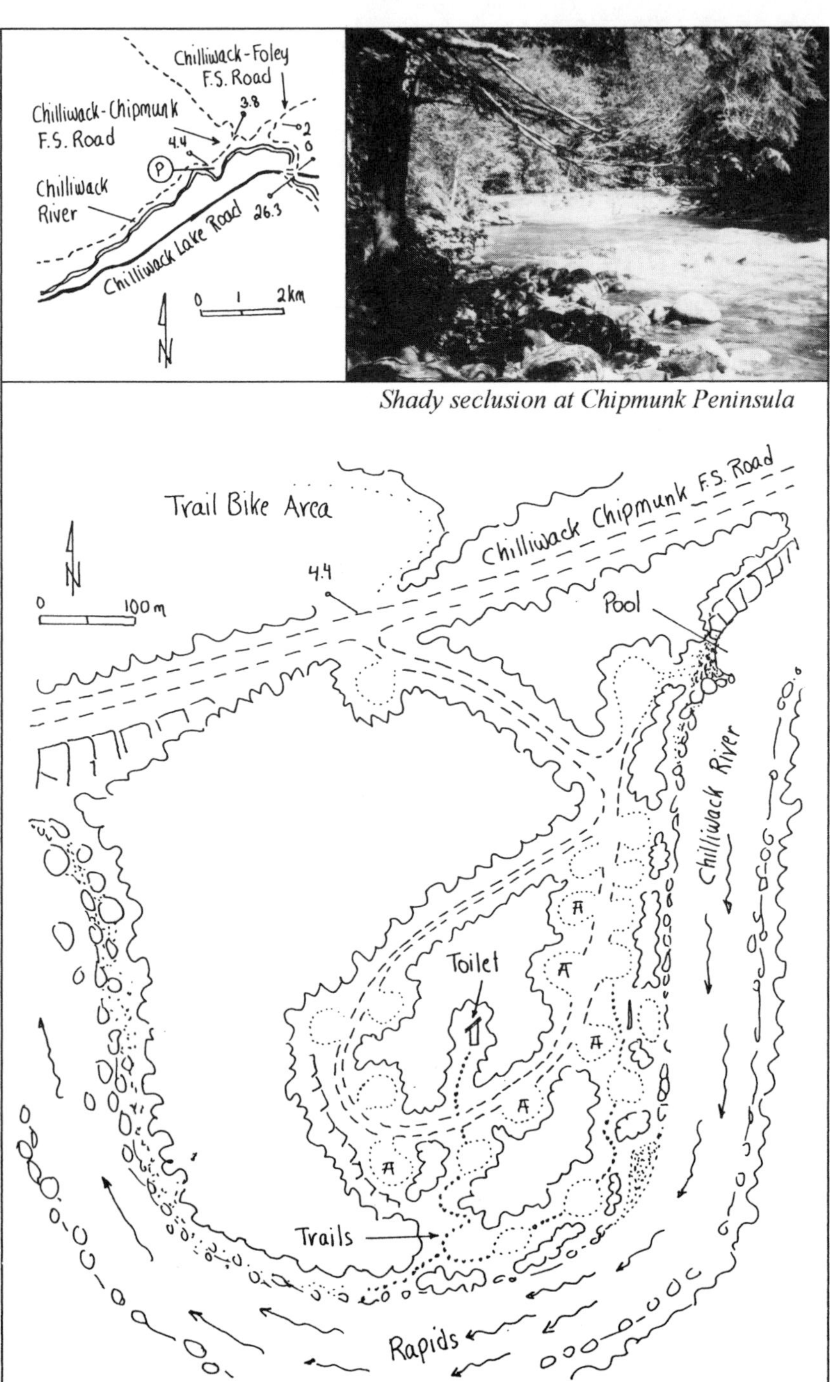

Shady seclusion at Chipmunk Peninsula

RAPIDS 29

- ☑ FISHING
- ☑ WHITE WATER
- ☑ RECREATION VEHICLES
- ☑ KAYAKING
- ☑ TENT CAMPING
- ☑ SMALL SITE

Quite appropriately named, this tiny site is situated beside the Chilliwack River where it has just finished gushing out of the narrow canyon and is scurrying frantically along a long incline. From this site you have a good view a long way upstream, a chance to view those desperate kayakers looking for a place to beach. A very small site, Rapids is a place that offers just a few picturesque camping spots beside the roaring white water.

White water and a shady place to rest

FINDING the SITE Take the Chilliwack Lake Road from Vedder Road south of Vedder Crossing for 26.3 kilometers. Just as you cross the Chilliwack River you will encounter the Chilliwack-Foley forest service road on the left. Turn left and zero out the odometer. At 2.0 kilometers cross the bridge over Foley Creek and make a turn left on the Chilliwack-Chipmunk Road. At 3.8 kilometers continue straight through ignoring the Chipmunk forest service road. At 4.4 kilometers a road peels off to the left into Chipmunk Peninsula.

Continue straight through until 7.0 kilometers where you will notice that you have come down to the river level and a short road cutting back to the left. This short road terminates at the Rapids site on the river bank.

SITE DESCRIPTION A very small site that will support only a few campers, the open gravel area adjoins a cleared area under a few tall timbers. A lone picnic table sits invitingly beside the river shore. There is a biffy at the end of the open area. A trail heads up stream from the site, paralleling the bank. Another pleasant little camp area is situated to the left as you drive in. This one has a tiny stream trickling beside it. That's it. Just below the road, a short path cuts down to a set of large flat rocks jutting into the river, forcing a slight bend to the river's path. From here you get a great view upstream and find out why the place is called Rapids.

SPECIAL FEATURES and ATTRACTIONS We visited this place in summer. Even then during low water there was no doubt about why it is called Rapids. During higher water the river forms a torrent of water through this channel. At this point the river has just finished its surge through the canyon a short distance upstream and then tumbles in a white water sequence for about a kilometer, down past the site. A kayaker would find this run particularly appealing, as would a rafter, but experience is an essential partner. Most of this run is not particularly deep, constantly rolling at a rather furious rate over large rocks. This is a particularly dangerous stretch for crunching knees or fiberglass. The exception is the canyon back further where the water is deeper but it is still treacherous.

As a pick-up point or camping spot to head for, this destination is perfect. There are two BCFS sites up stream to launch from, at Camp Foley and at Chipmunk Peninsula. These were described earlier. The challenge here is to know where to beach if no-one is waving a flag on shore for you.

There are also a few other attractions in this area. The Cheam Trail which extends from the end of the Chipmunk forest service road, is an unsurpassed trail to hike but you need a 4X4 to get there. If no 4X4 is available you can hike the more sedate Centennial Trail starting from its east end. It is 1.6 kilometers past the Eagles Roost site described next.

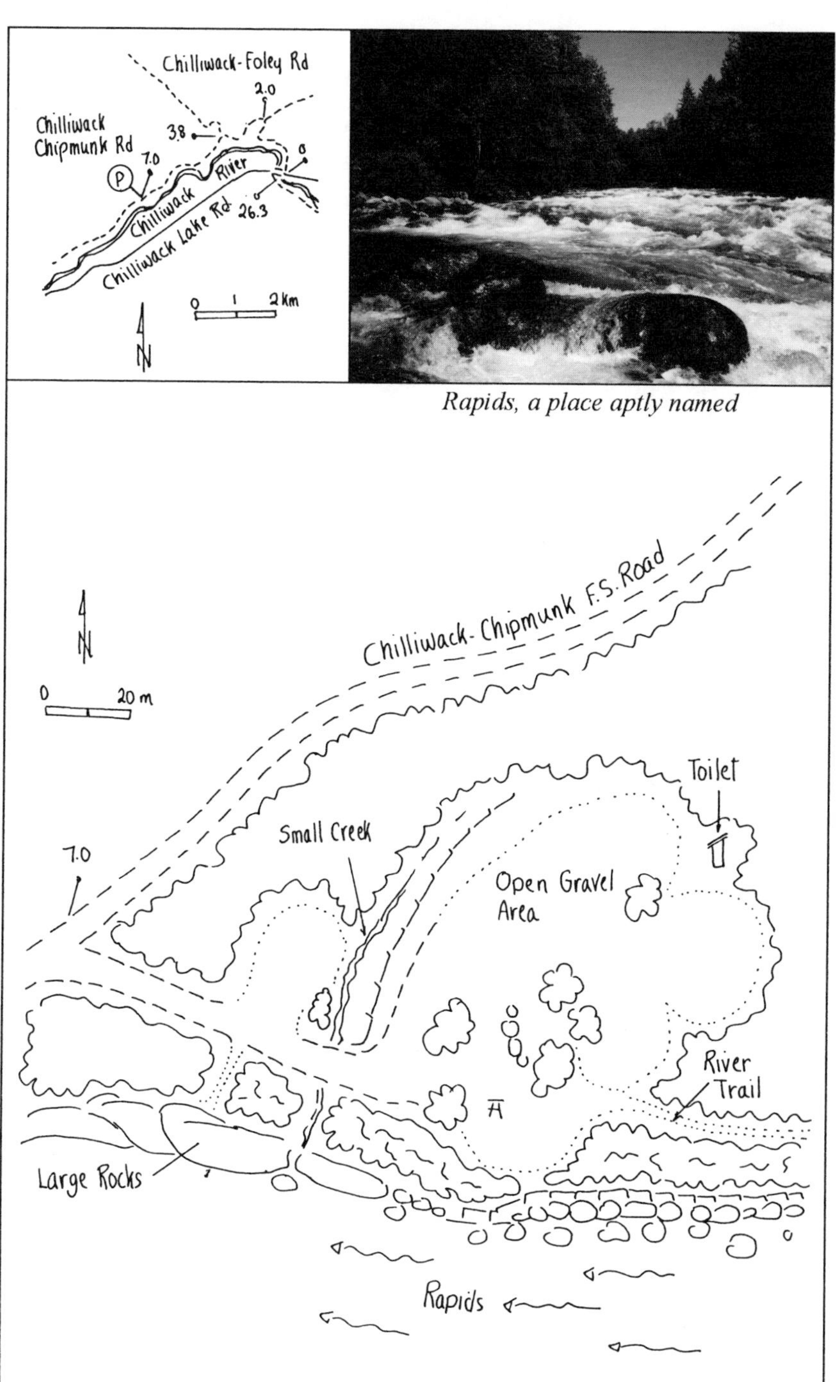

Rapids, a place aptly named

EAGLES ROOST 30

- ☑ WHITE WATER
- ☑ RUBBER RAFTING
- ☑ RECREATION VEHICLES
- ☑ KAYAKING
- ☑ TENT CAMPING
- ☑ SMALL SITE

This small site will not make you leap for your camera but it is definitely a nice quiet shaded spot that will invite you to pitch tent or pull out the picnic pack. Sitting on a bench above a thin branch of the Chilliwack River, this place, called Eagles Roost is anything but a place for eagles... perhaps there must be something that I missed.

A small but quiet site by the river

FINDING the SITE Access is by car. Take the Chilliwack Lake Road from Vedder Road south of Vedder Crossing for 26.3 kilometers. Just as you cross the Chilliwack River you will encounter the Chilliwack-Foley forest service road on the left. Turn left and zero out the odometer. At 2.0 kilometers cross the bridge over Foley Creek and make a turn left on the Chilliwack-Chipmunk Road. At 3.8 kilometers continue straight through ignoring the Chipmunk forest service road. At 4.4 kilometers a road peels off to the left into

Chipmunk Peninsula. Continue straight through to 7.8 kilometers where you break out into an open bank and the site on the left.

SITE DESCRIPTION Not particularly well endowed with camping pads, the site still has all the usual BCFS facilities. The central biffy, a couple of fire rings, and a lone picnic table service about 5 pads sitting strategically in the shade trees. The flat area, easily accessed, is situated on a flat bench beside a smaller split in the river so most of the site fronts the river, allowing easy access to the river via a short meter drop. Just a wee bit upstream in the woods you will find a secluded area with a tiny gravel beach. Because of the close proximity to the road, the U-shaped entry-exit allows a camper or trailer to be brought in easily.

SPECIAL FEATURES and ATTRACTIONS I am not entirely sure of the real attraction at this site, particularly with reference to its name of Eagles Roost. Although this eludes me, let it be said the site is a quiet and refreshing spot to relax. The Centennial and Cheam Peak trails are within easy reach for those who like a hike, offering an easy hike along the Chilliwack River or a more spectacular hike up to 2112 meters at Cheam. If you have kept track of distance, the Centennial trailhead is at 9.4 kilometers (1.6 past Eagles Roost) and the Chipmunk road was at 3.8 kilometers.

If you have been reading the previous sites down this strip of road you will have noted that the feature has been the kayaking down the river. Thus Camp Foley, Chipmunk Peninsula, and Rapids were pick-up or destination points. This site could also serve the same purpose but you would have to know where the little branch cuts off the river to the Eagles Roost bank. Otherwise, you may want to consider stationing a buddy with a flag at the river's bank to mark the landing spot. After this, if you miss the beaching, you will have no more chances to get picked up on this side of the river.

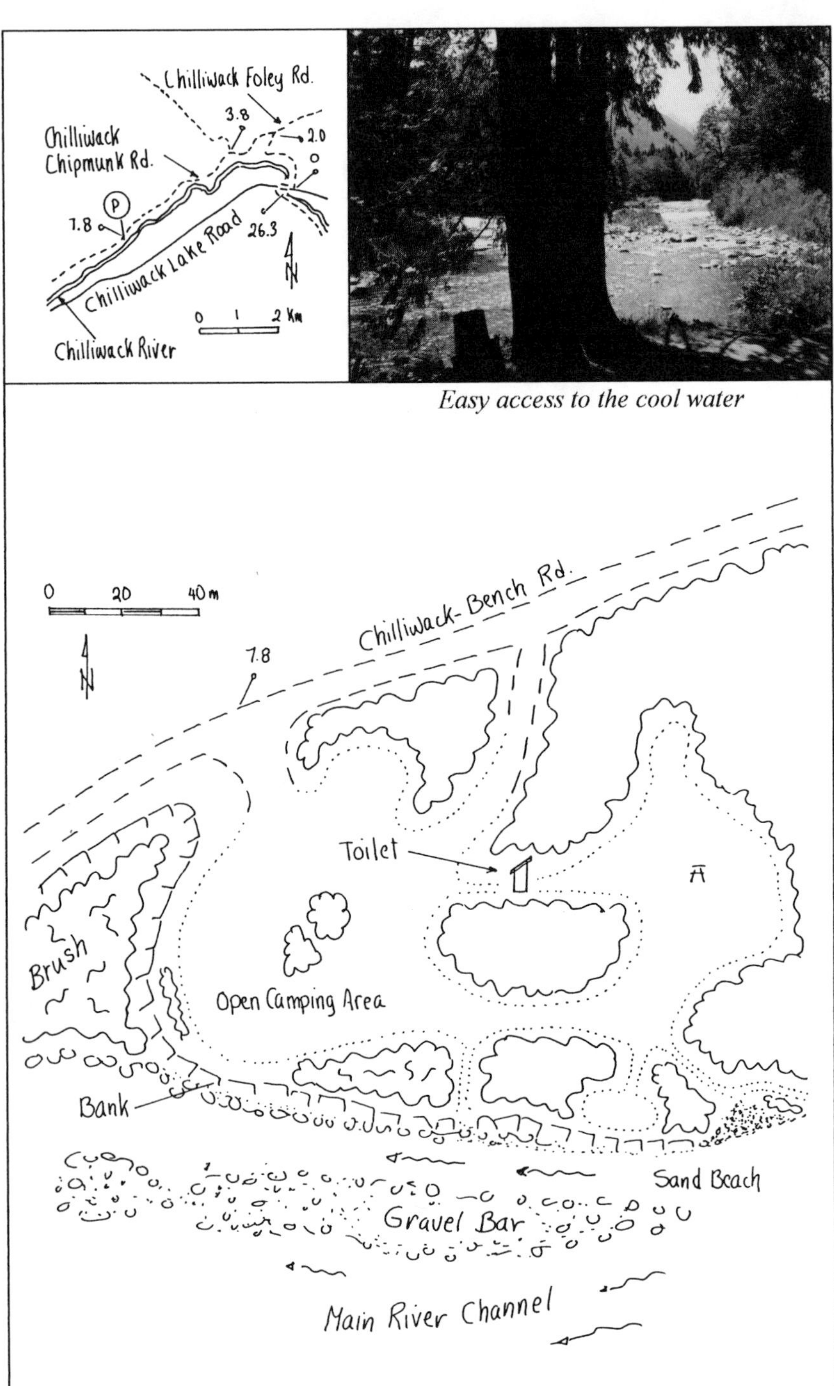

Easy access to the cool water

FOLEY LAKE 31

- ☑ TRAIL BIKING
- ☑ CANOEING
- ☑ FISHING
- ☑ TENT CAMPING
- ☑ RECREATION VEHICLES
- ☑ MEDIUM SITE

This site sits on one of the most unusual looking lakes in the valley. Depending on your viewpoint you can get absolute opposite impressions of this lake. From the west end looking up the Foley Valley you will see a postcard perfect scene of a lake against a magnificent backdrop of mountains. From the southeast you will see an eerie scene of broken-off logs poking out of the lake surface creating a most peculiar contrast of dead trees against a shoreline of lush vegetation. Trapped between a long narrow canyon, the waters of Foley Lake will take your breath away or make you feel uncomfortable... like something weird happened here. The odd thing is that this lake has a magical mix of clutter and serenity, offering a mix of shady camp pads, quiet canoe waters, with evening fish that dot the water as they rise.

An eerie mix in the morning mist

FINDING the SITE Take the Chilliwack Lake Road for 26.3 kilometers from the Vedder Road. At this point, just as you cross the Chilliwack River, leave the pavement and turn left onto the Chilliwack-Foley forest service road. If you zero your odometer here it is a mere 6.2 kilometers along a good gravel road so don't fret about your Porsche. Besides testing the shocks on the pot-holes it will be fine. At 2.0 kilometers keep right and follow Foley Creek all the way to 6.2 kilometers where you will see a small parking area and the familiar brown stake marking the west campsite on the left. The road continues along the shore of the lake and splits at 6.6 kilometers. The left fork cuts down to Foley Creek but just before the creek an obscure road cuts back along the bank to the east campsites. Sorry but your Porsche won't like this road. It is a few hundred meters to the open gravel area serving as a parking lot. The east camp-sites are found here on a small grassy bench overlooking the lake. From here there are a few short trails to shore.

SITE DESCRIPTION There are two small BCFS campsites. The south-west site is the largest with about seven main pads sitting nicely in the tall timbers overlooking the lake. From the parking area the bank drops down into some second growth timbers, dominating the round rocky outcrop area mostly bare of underbrush. There are several picnic tables here, a biffy and several fire rings. Access to the shore is easy, allowing you to carry a canoe or small boat to the water. Below this, at the west end of the lake, it is cluttered and muddy with large craggy boulders along the shore. This is where Foley Creek pours through the narrow exit end of the lake forcing logs and debris to clutter it.

To the right, or east, this muddy and unfriendly shoreline gives way to a nice sandy beach strip at about mid-lake. If a canoe is your pleasure, this beach is a perfect launch area. There are also a few prime camping pads along the beach. It is a pretty spot set down from the road shaded by tall timbers.

The east end campsites are accessed via a little rough road that drops down and cuts back below the main road to a small bench. Here you find a small parking lot, biffy and a few campsites beside a grassy area. Shore access requires a three-meter drop to the lake. From here the view is eerie as the camp site looks out through the tall timbers at the deadheads, a strange but appealing view. The northeast shore is a gravel/sand bar but access is not simple, demanding a boat. A unique feature is that adjacent to this bar, Williamson Creek pours its waters directly into the lake in a 10 meter fall. This particular sand bar has become a popular area where you can sun and fish.

SPECIAL FEATURES and ATTRACTIONS Foley Lake is the main attraction here. It is a reasonably high lake at 550 meters but it is still very easy to get to. This 11-hectare lake is a particularly interesting one for the fisherman.

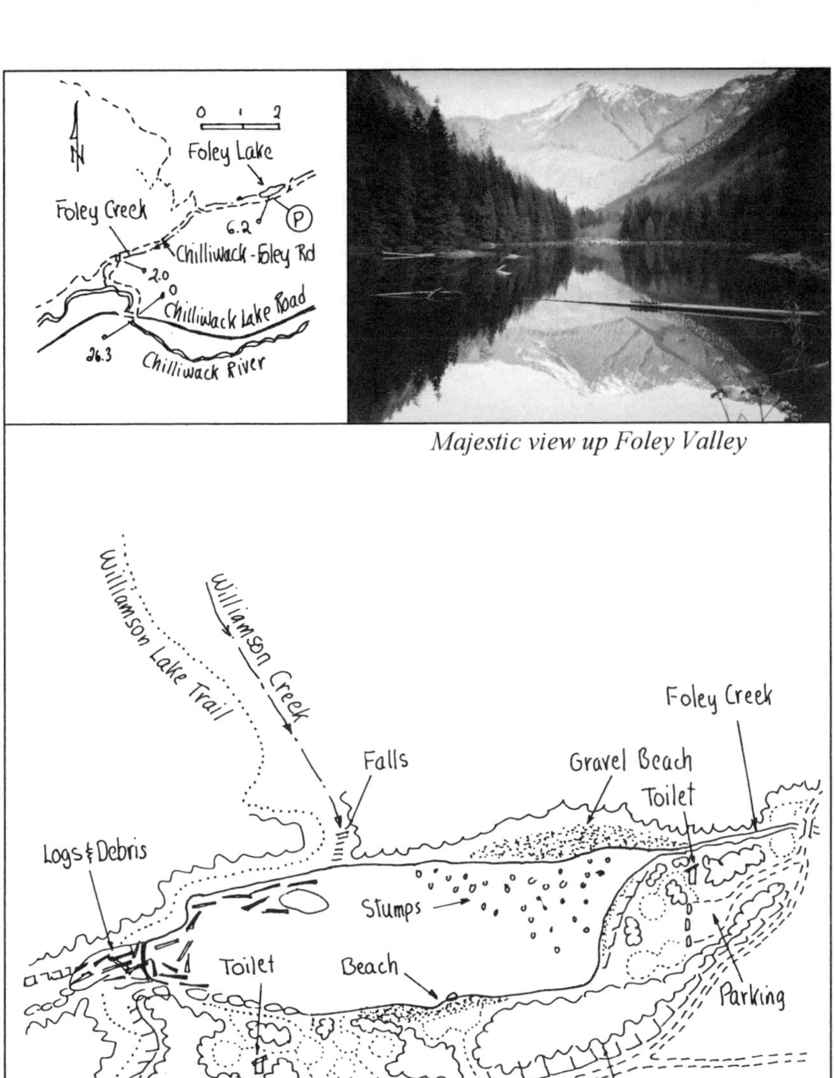

Majestic view up Foley Valley

The lake contains dollys and 25- to 35-centimeter trout. When you first see this lake you will know right away there are some beauties here. The creek circulates the water well; there is a fair amount of shade and it is full of logs and stumps offering fish a good place to hide or escape. The water is clear and dark, containing a good supply of algae. Shore access to the lake is best at the south beach area. The lake has been stocked placing 1500 rainbow of catchable size in the lake each year from 1986 to 1990. No power boats (except for electric motors) are allowed making it an absolute dream for canoeing. At 550 meters elevation, the lake is reasonably high, trapping mists on the water quite often. Slipping your canoe silently through the mist at dawn, between those rising trout is shear magic to a fly fisherman.

Trail biking If you want to explore the area there are many old and newer logging roads in the area. The system that continues up Foley Creek has several spur roads climbing high up on the ridges, as does the system below the lake. The Airplane Ridge system of roads found before Foley Lake also provides a vast network to explore.

Williamson Lake and trail is another attraction, a mere two hectares in size but its elevation of 1650 meters makes it a challenge to get to. The lake is in a small flat plateau technically in the permanent snow-line high above Foley Lake. Of significance is that this lake borders on alpine terrain and if you can endure the hike you will get a taste for some unique terrain and seldom seen vegetation. A summer hike only, the area is probably missing snow only a few months of the year but the lake has another unique aspect to it; the area is a natural habitat for mountain goats. Unfortunately, visiting hikers have had an impact on the goat population in that they have disturbed the natural order of things. Reports are that the goats are slowly leaving the area so hiking this trail is discouraged. Originally put in by a hiking club who had good intentions, the trail is now in rough shape and not well marked so it is a very tough climb.

From the west Foley Lake site there is a small open gravel area back about 200 meters. The trail is rather obscure so find and follow the small culvert under the road. You may even see orange ribbons on the tree. The trail dives into the debris along the ditch bed to the end of Foley Lake where the creek has accumulated so much debris that in summer you can walk across the junk to the other side. The trail follows the lakeshore for about 400 meters then turns to parallel Williamson Creek where the ascent begins. When you have covered a mere two kilometers from the road, you will have climbed to the ridge at an elevation of 1400 meters. If you are quiet you may see the goats. From here things level for only .5 kilometers and the climb starts again taking you to the lake at 1650 meters for a total distance of 3.6 kilometers.

RIVERSIDE 32

☑ HIKING
☑ SMALL SITE
☑ TENT CAMPING
☑ TRAIL BIKING

So what, you will say after reading the above features, is the attraction here? Admittedly not much of a list, and adding hiking to the list is not exactly true since this is not part of the site, but I must come to this site's defense. Here tall Douglas firs dominate the long bench along the Chilliwack River. They let nothing else but their species live here. They stand like sentinels guarding their selected family members, completely blocking the sun with their needle canopy, creating a rather magical setting for a campsite. The roar of the river and the wind in the trees add to the feeling that you are completely isolated, in a deep forest, even though the road is 100 meters away. It is really a small place but it offers a mix of natural sensations that will make you feel very peaceful. Try stopping for a picnic.

The guarding timbers at Riverside

FINDING the SITE Access is via the Chilliwack Lake Road off of Vedder Road. At exactly 29.5 kilometers along the Chilliwack Lake Road you will see a pullout into the trees on the right side of the road. This side road curves in a large arc, paralleling the Chilliwack River bank for .5 kilometers before it emerges at the main road again. The site stretches along this loop. Recently the Forestry blocked access to the site so it would not suffer from over population and over-zealous hooligans. You have to park at either end, the farthest end having the most room.

SITE DESCRIPTION On either side of the short access road through the site you will find several open camping pads. Although about 10 are clearly demarcated as pads, the area is naked of underbrush making it possible to pitch a tent just about anywhere. There is a central biffy and you will find metal fire rings placed at most pads. The sites are distributed all along the road with a few (probably unofficial) nice spots on the two peninsulas poking out into the river.

SPECIAL FEATURES and ATTRACTIONS At this particular spot, the river makes a slight bend forming a wide, flat bench between the road and the river bank. The river rushes by the full length below a short 1-2 meter bank. The tall timbers appear to love this spot so much so that nothing else is allowed to grow here. Needless to say, the scene is indeed unique since a view down road from either end of the site resembles a long tunnel from an adventure scene, the path taunting you onwards into the lost world of sinister timbers watching your actions. Interestingly enough, both road and river are almost hidden so even though you are close to the road, you see little of it.

Hiking There are several neat trails close by the site. Ford Mountain Trail is back at 28.4 km. and the Williams Ridge Trail is a bit further on across the road at 32.2 km.

The Ford Mountain Trail is found by taking the Ford Mountain forestry road at exactly 28.4 kilometers. This road looks reasonably respectable but it rises almost immediately to start its climb from 400 meters at the start to 1020 meters at the trailhead. The road is in reasonable shape, with a few deep ditches requiring decent (truck) clearance but the steepness will demand 4X4 traction in several places. If you are able to drive to the trailhead you will have saved 4.3 kilometers and 620 meters of elevation gain, roughly 2.5 hours. There is a small parking lot at the bottom if you do not have an appropriate vehicle. Alternatively you can drive to the Williams Ridge Trail 3.8 kilometers farther along Chilliwack Lake Road and climb the short-cut straight up the ridge. The footpath starts at elevation 1020 meters and rises steeply through thick forest to the northeast and the ridge, elevation 1250 meters. From here the trail continues to climb slowly along the ridge, still in trees, to the little knob where the lookout used to be. Only remnants of the old lookout will be found here. From here, elevation 1421 meters, the trail continues all the way to Williams Peak, 6 kilometers from the Ford Lookout, after passing the Williams Ridge Trail (at

0 1 2km
N
Chilliwack Foley
F.S. Road
26.3
29.5
P
Chilliwack River
Chilliwack Lake
Road

RYCHKUN

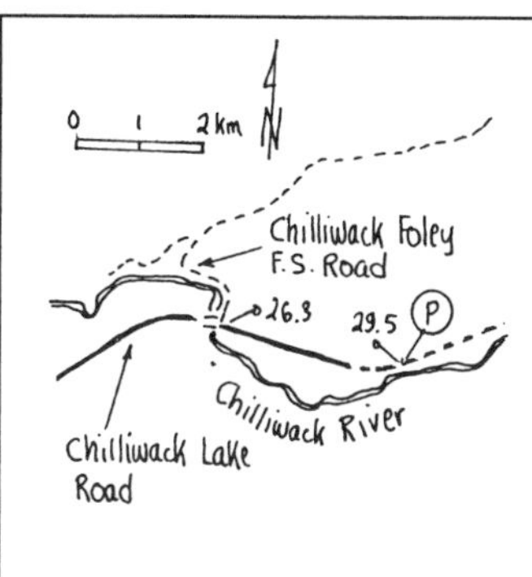

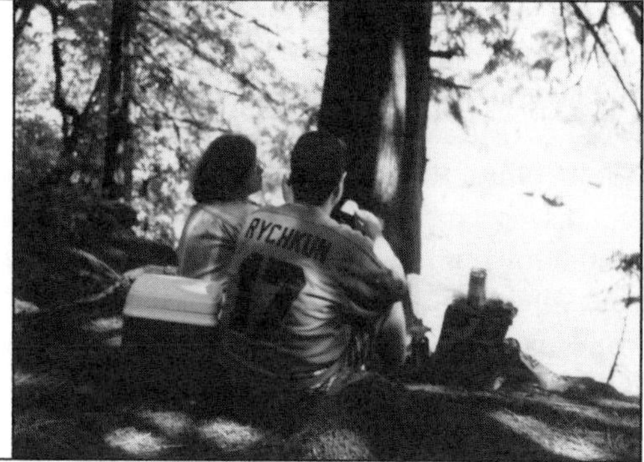

Relaxing at Riverside

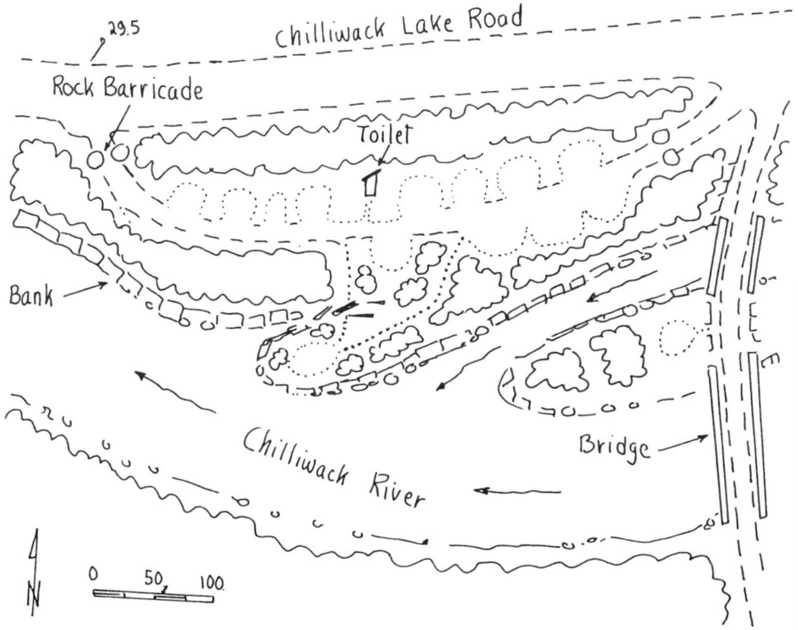

29.5
Chilliwack Lake Road
Rock Barricade
Toilet
Bank
Chilliwack River
Bridge
N
0 50 100

2.3 kilometers along the ridge from the Lookout). The elevation gain is moderate keeping you at around 1500 along the ridge. The last 2 kilometers to Williams Peak rises rapidly to 1880 meters.

The *Williams Ridge Trail* is at 32.2 km. Here a short access road heads north and disappears into the trees. It is marked by the BCFS post. The actual trailhead is a few hundred meters in where the BCFS survey post marks the beginning of the footpath. It is on the left, slightly obscured by the thick bush. From the trailhead at an elevation of 400 meters, you head west then north, following the orange markers carefully. The trail now starts to rise. At 500 meters in, you will have gained 100 meters in elevation. But the next 1.7 kilometers rises mercilessly back and forth lifting 300 meters for every 500 horizontal meters. At 1 kilometer you pass the creek tributaries, (800 meters elevation). The climb now lifts to 1400 meters in elevation at the ridge, 2.2 kilometers from the car. Here you will encounter the ridge trail. From this point, left takes you to Ford Mountain Lookout, 2.3 kilometers away and right takes you 3.8 kilometers to Williams Peak. Taking the right (east) path, the ridge becomes relatively flat, much of which is still wooded. You will continue to follow the ridge northeast past the knoll to the 4 kilometer mark (from the car). From here, if you dare, you start the second ascent to the grand finale'.

You will always see the peculiar peak sticking out like a cinder cone in the distance, goading you on. As you open out into the rocky meadow you approach the thrust of rock which requires a special effort to climb. ***This is not the official trail... it ended at an elevation of 1880 meters.*** The peak is actually at 2080 meters! If you decide to take the challenge, be equipped and be careful... there is no help up here. The approach is to the right along the lower base and up the south wall. From this point you will be able to see Foley Peak and the glaciers to the northwest.

POST CREEK 33

☑ HIKING
☑ MEDIUM SITE
☑ TENT CAMPING
☑ RECREATION VEHICLES

This is a very popular spot in the summer. The reason is that it serves as overflow from the Chilliwack Lake provincial park. It also provides a trailhead hub for several exceptional trails. On top of this it is easily accessible by car and it has its very own desirable features. Picture a babbling stream to wade in, rustling alders, cool fresh air, tall firs swaying in the breeze, open rolling terrain splattered with moss and salal... sure you've heard this before but this is a very peaceful stream setting. The combination makes this a popular place. If you can come here for a visit, keep away from a weekend and stay on the less busy western side so you also may have a chance to appreciate it.

A shady, cool place to pitch camp

FINDING the SITE Since the recreation site straddles Post Creek, there are two access points both off Chilliwack Lake Road. To get to the west side of the creek zero out at Vedder Road and Chilliwack Lake Road. Drive for 38.3 kilometers and turn left into the trees on a gravel road. The forestry sign should mark the road. This is a potholed but level road ending at the west side of the creek. If you drive slow, your car will hopefully keep its muffler. The second entry is at 39 kilometers where you will see another sign marking the Centennial Trail. Take this gravel road for one kilometer to the end and the parking lot. This also serves as a parking lot for two BCFS trails.

SITE DESCRIPTION The campsites are set nicely beside the creek in the shade, with the majority of these being on the west side. They are distributed along the bank of the stream on rocky outcrop or set back from creek frontage on the road. On the west side, the main parking area is at the end of the road but another small place is found just south on the campsite extension. A few picnic tables can be found at the choice pads. There are garbage cans and a biffy for the westerners. A well constructed foot bridge crosses over the stream connecting this side to the eastern section.

On the east side there are also some super spots but the big problem is the large parking lot which can become seriously congested. This lot serves as the hiker's parking place to Lindeman, Flora and Greendrop lakes, sometimes making it difficult for any eastern residents to maneuver or get some peace and quiet... and there are some really nice spots here. On this side, there are garbage cans and a biffy hidden in the trees. The camping area is more open here with fewer demarcated pads. If the east side is full, drive back down to the 38.3 kilometer mark and the road will take you to the other side.

SPECIAL FEATURES and ATTRACTIONS In addition to its serene wooded-stream setting, the site offers some other attractions. It provides a base camp for exploring the rest of the area via some excellent trail systems.

Hiking trails There are two fantastic hiking trails accessible directly from the site. The first is the Post Greendrop Trail which takes you to two beautiful lakes, Lindeman and Greendrop while the second, Flora Lake Trail takes you to Flora Lake.

The *Post Greendrop Trail* will start the climb from 650 meters in elevation at the site's east parking lot. You will ascend briskly through the timbers to cross the creek on an unusual log bridge. At about 800 meters distance you begin to flatten the climb. At about 1.0 kilometer you will be at the crest of the valley where it levels off to the lake elevation of 838 meters. It is another short 200 meters to the south end of the lake. This south end has a large open area at lakeshore suitable for camping... but no facilities. The trail continues over the rock talus along the west shore to the north end of the lake where you have access to a gravel beach area... another camping area with no facilities. From the trailhead it is only 35 minutes to the south end of Lindeman, about an hour to the north end (2 kilometers from the car).

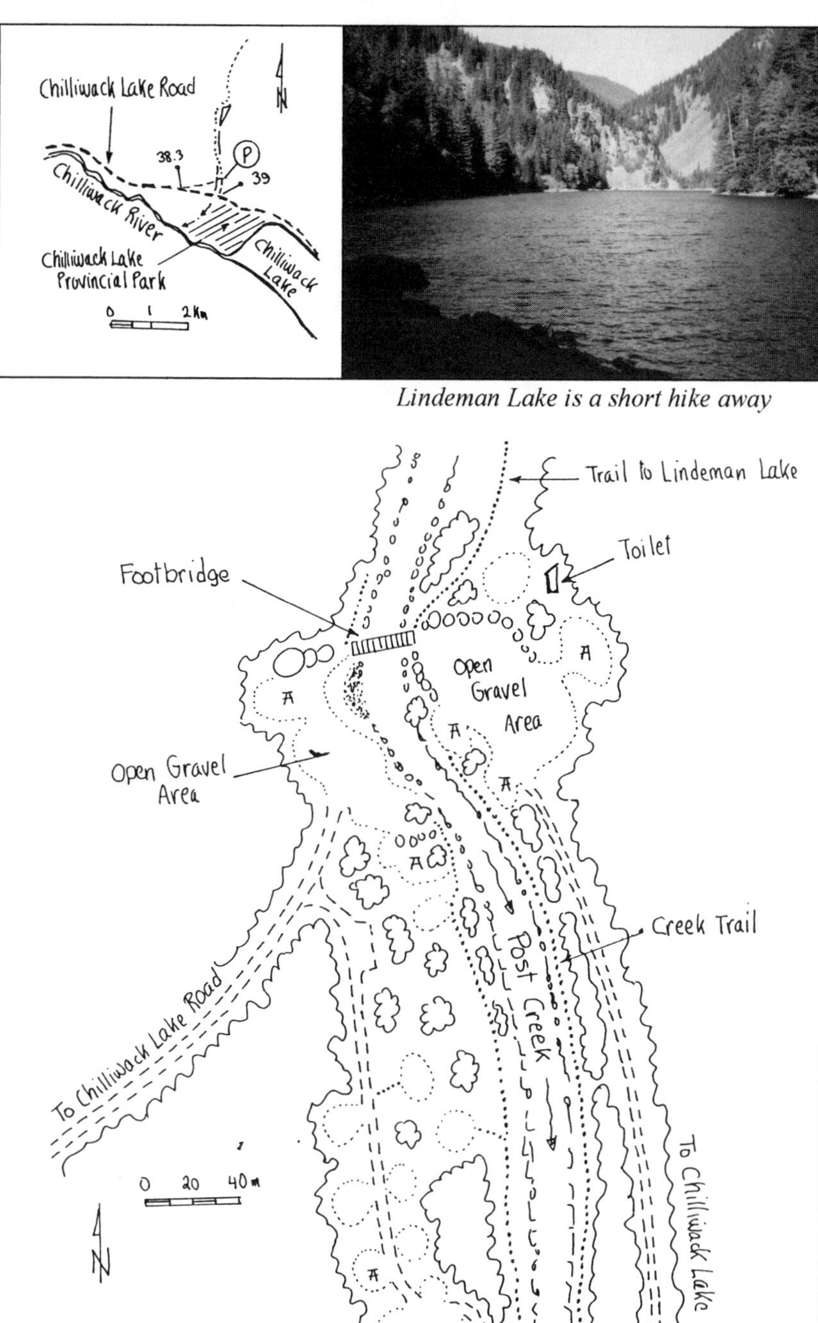

Lindeman Lake is a short hike away

From the north end of Lindeman, the trail then continues up the creek to Greendrop Lake. Follow Post Creek, climbing to an elevation of 910 meters over the next kilometer. The ascent is gradual but there are several places where you need to climb over boulders and talus thus slowing the pace. This part is not an easy stroll. At about 3.6 kilometers you cross over to the northwest side of the creek and finally encounter a branch trail at five kilometers. The right branch takes you to the natural picnic area and campsite at the south end of the lake. The left branch continues up above the lake on to Skagit Valley. Once again, there are no facilities. The elevation is now 1021 meters and the total distance is 5.2 kilometers. The total one-way trip should be possible in three hours.

The *Flora Lake Trail* is found back from the site along the access road. From the sign on the road you will climb up to the ridge, at an unforgiving pace, starting from an elevation of 650 meters gaining about 1125 meters vertically in five kilometers. You make the final assault on the pass at an elevation of 1775 meters. Once on the ridge, you can climb a bit higher if you wish to look in all directions. You may even be satisfied and decide to turn back. From here you will drop just as steeply into the Flora Lake Valley, going down just a wee bit over 416 meters vertically—a fairly tough hike for most non-Olympic athletes. If you intend to do it as a day walk, remember going back is just as tough and the total length *one way* is 7 kilometers so allow five to six hours to get there. You will reach the south end of the lake near the entry stream. It is probably a good idea to plan an overnight expedition.

In addition just across the road is the Post Creek cross country trail system that will lead you to the Radium Lake Trail. The cross country trails are the easiest letting you saunter through the flat bushes near the creek. Radium, covered earlier, is probably between post Greendrop and Flora for difficulty. All of these can be done in a day's outing, easily accessed from the site.

Chilliwack Lake is situated close to the site. If you continue down the Chilliwack Lake Road from the Post Creek turnoff, a vast waterway opens up to you within minutes. The road hugs the shore for about 10 kilometers offering access points to the water and some unforgettable post card quality scenes. It is the largest lake in the region measuring 1198 hectares. At 620 meters in elevation the lake has characteristically cool and clear water even in mid summer.

With an easily accessible eastern lakeshore, this lake is impressive; a vast body of water essentially untouched except for the logging roads following the eastern shore. There is still little sign of any commercial clutter. Surprisingly, the lake has been spared from development so it all looks natural. With the development of the excellent facilities at the provincial park and the facilities provided by the Forest Service at the south end, the lake offers an extensive list of recreational facilities. Camping is a highlight, as are fishing, boating and hiking. You will want to stay a while, particularly off-season in the fall or spring.

Post Creek Cross-Country Ski Trails It is worth mentioning the cross-country ski trails constructed by the Federation of Mountain Clubs of BC. The Post Creek Cross-Country Ski Trails measure about 7.5 kilometers in total and cover a variety of terrain within a relatively small area. The trails are designed to cover a range of abilities, including beginners, intermediate and advanced skiers. All are marked with color-coded directional signs according to ability. These are found on the other side of the main Chilliwack Lake Road opposite the Post Creek recreation site.

Chilliwack Lake Provincial Park is at the north end of the lake. I mention this simply because the Post Creek site is just opposite the road from this park. You will find a long list of less rustic conveniences and excellent boat access to the beautiful Chilliwack Lake. It is certainly a better endowed camping area set nicely in a short stubby pine forest. This place has an impressive layout of some 100 campsites, the best ones close to the lake. The park is well-endowed with pit toilets, water and firewood, a playground, a small day-use area and several trails that link with the regional ones. The boat launch is of good quality, with a parking lot for trailers and a beach area around it.

PALEFACE CREEK 34

- ☑ BEACH
- ☑ CANOEING
- ☑ FISHING
- ☑ BOAT LAUNCH
- ☑ BOATING
- ☑ TENT CAMPING
- ☑ SWIMMING
- ☑ RECREATION VEHICLES
- ☑ TRAIL BIKING
- ☑ SMALL SITE

At first glance Paleface doesn't look too appealing but if you stop to inspect the area that the site is scattered about on, you will begin to change your mind. Being close to the main road also gives the place a bit of a blemish. But if you are lucky enough to find a camping pad at the lower end where the site is secluded, usually off season or off weekends, you will surely enjoy this place. Situated on the east side of Chilliwack Lake, this site is made up of two parts, the camping area along Paleface Creek and the boat launch on Chilliwack Lake, close to where the creek enters the lake. Together these two spots will let you camp, fish, boat, beach and swim.

Paleface Creek boat launch on Chilliwack Lake

FINDING the SITE The north end of Chilliwack Lake is reached by car by driving 39.4 kilometers from Vedder Road along the Chilliwack Lake Road

At this point a sign marks the provincial park entrance. From here the road continues along the lakeshore changing its name to the Chilliwack Lake forest service road. It actually parallels the east shore of the lake all the way to the end. The road deteriorates gradually but you can get your car all the way to the end of the lake. The Paleface Creek boat launch is found at 46.5 kilometers, where a small parking lot on the right is found after a short gravel road drop to the boat launch. The Paleface campsite is around the corner at 46.9 kilometers, just past the launch. A short road drops to a slight bench along the creek where you find the camping pads.

SITE DESCRIPTION The site is split into two parts. The first site on the left at 46.5 kilometers is the official boat launch. A small parking lot on the main road is found just past the short steep turn-off to the lakeshore and launch. The boat launch is made of concrete cross-slabs, a bit steep, thereby limiting your ability to launch with a big trailer. There are also a few places that serve as informal campsites. There is a small place to park a few vehicles at the bottom but the main parking area is by the upper road. The lone biffy stands across from the main road and you will find a nice beach area at the exit of Paleface Creek-when the water in the lake is low.

The main camping section is positioned between the road and the boulder strewn Paleface Creek around the bend from the launch area. The camping pads are distributed along a narrow bench, positioned nicely beneath tall fir trees, numbering about 12, looking out over the creek. This is a nice wooded setting open and cleared of underbrush. Some of the pads being placed under some enormous firs, all easily accessed. There is a pair of biffies here but little else. From the west end of the site you are able to drop down via a good path to the lake and a gravel beach, its size being dependent on the water level in the lake. There is also a private camping pad at the top end, accessed via a short access road down to the creek just before you cross the Paleface bridge.

SPECIAL FEATURES and ATTRACTIONS Chilliwack Lake is the main feature here. The Paleface site is a bit past the midpoint of the lake, along the gravel road that hugs the shore for about 10 kilometers. The deep green placid water and the mountain backdrops provide some unforgettable postcard quality scenes. It is the largest lake in the region measuring 1198 hectares. At 620 meters in elevation the lake has characteristically cool and clear water even in mid summer. An easily accessible eastern lakeshore, makes this lake an excellent recreation place.

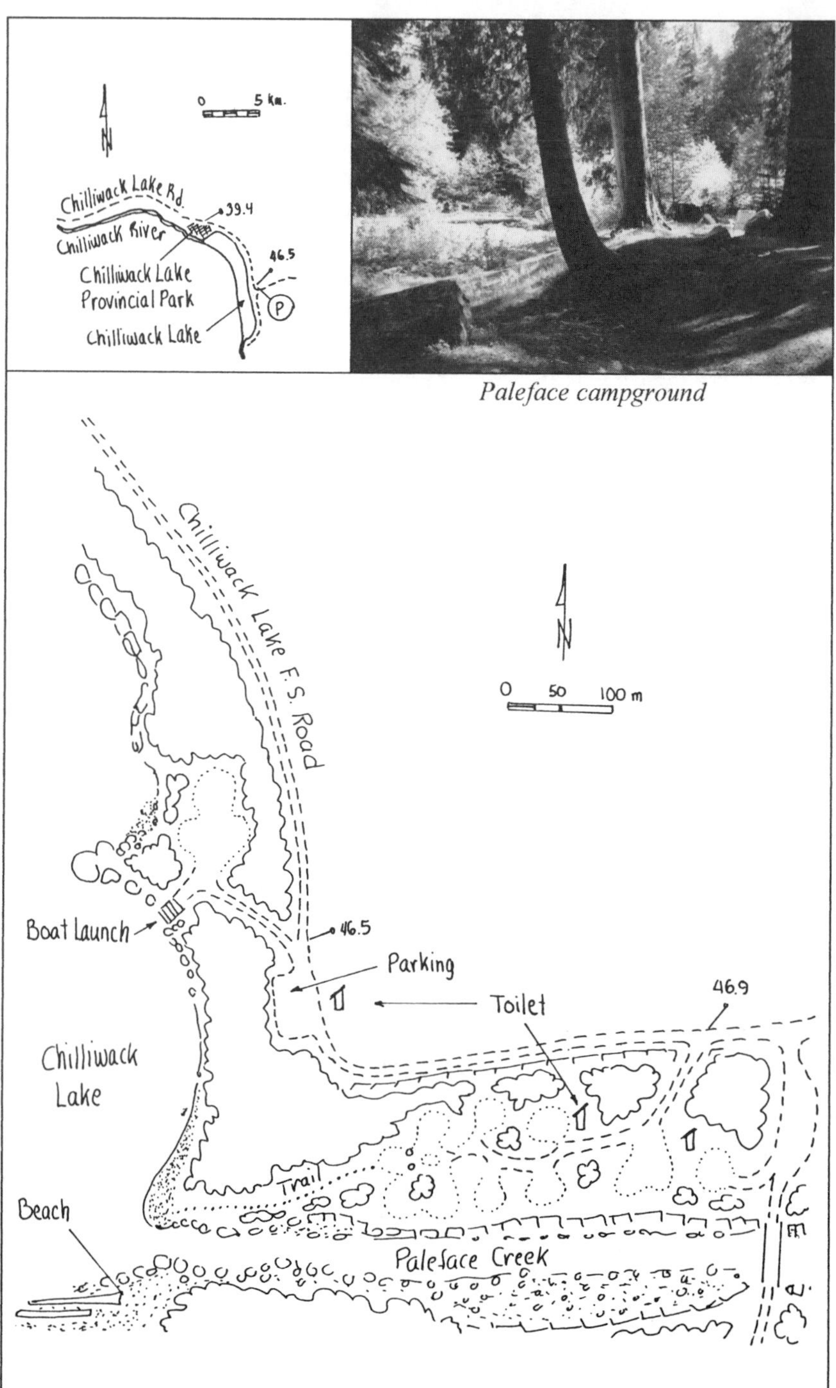

Paleface campground

There is still little sign of any commercial clutter. Surprisingly, the lake has been spared from development so it all looks natural. Camping is a highlight, as are fishing and boating and hiking.

Trail biking In addition, the logging road system in this area is quite extensive reaching deep up Paleface and Depot creeks (see next site). These also lead to numerous spur roads taking you well up into the mountains, an excellent venue for dirt biking and exploring.

DEPOT CREEK 35

- ☑ BEACH
- ☑ FISHING
- ☑ RECREATION VEHICLES
- ☑ TENT CAMPING
- ☑ SWIMMING
- ☑ SMALL SITE

Although it doesn't look great from the road, once you drive down into this place the magic setting will transform your initial impression. As you drive down through the scruffy forest and into the main site, the park-like setting of open timbers, the shady camp pads below the deep green canopy will reveal themselves. Glimpses of the blue lake waters highlighting the soft sandy beach will force an adrenaline rush. The Depot Creek site is situated on a large gravel projection into the Chilliwack Lake. It is one of the prettiest spots on the lake. This whole area has been created by massive piles of gravel that has obviously invaded the lake over time as Depot Creek alternates from a raging torrent in run-off season to a more subdued stream in summer. As a result of the push, there is a massive gravel bar, cut in half by the creek, offering beaches on the south and north reaches. The main camping area, on the south reach, is in a nicely protected bay with its very own sandy beach.

Sandy beach behind the Depot Creek camping area

FINDING the SITE From the Vedder Road intersection south of Vedder Crossing take the Chilliwack Lake Road past the provincial park at 39.4 kilometers to hit the Chilliwack Lake forest service road. This road parallels the east shore of the lake all the way to the end. The road deteriorates gradually but you can get your car all the way to the end of the lake (well, almost). You will pass the Paleface Creek boat launch at 46.5 kilometers and the Paleface campsite at 46.9 kilometers. At 50.0 kilometers you will see an open gravel area before crossing Depot Creek. This is the *upper* Depot Creek site marking a poor road that takes you close to the north bay. You had a glimpse at it on the way in. This spot also serves as overflow camping and a parking lot in the event the gate at the bridge is closed. Because the main camping area is small and easily plugged by traffic, the forestry *may* decide to shut the gate at the bridge and you may need to park back on the other side of the bridge.

Assuming a drive through, at the 50.5 kilometer mark, just over the bridge on the right there is a short road that drops down into the lower forest. This road is only a few hundred meters long but it has a rough section at the top. Loose rocks and boulders may knock the oil pan off your Corvette... check it first. At the bottom, the road curls around in a loop providing access to the camp pads.

SITE DESCRIPTION There are about 15 camping pads, distributed around the loop. These sit in a shoreline strip of thick forest facing the south cove. The trees are so thick it is dark even when the sun is bright, completely preventing any brush from growing. The camp pads sit against the timbers giving most a nice shady backyard under the fir and cedar canopy, opening out to the beautiful backdrop of the lake, and the strip of beach (on the lake side of the loop). It is only 50 meters to the small sandy beach from the pads, thereby a small craft such as a canoe could be carried easily. If you have anything larger, it would need to be launched at Paleface Creek. On the opposite side of the loop road the pads are not as fine, set away from the beach area. There are two biffies and a gravel beach that extends all the way around the point. Wood is usually available.

For those fishermen who want to isolate themselves and fish off the large gravel bar, the choice may be to drive the truck to the end of the north access road and park in an area that will be distinctly rough. The road is flat but it winds through the forest with massive potholes and poking rocks that require a truck with high clearance. The road ends in the tangle of brush and debris where a rough "trail" has been trampled out over logs, branches, brush and tangled swamp to the shore. It is only 200 meters to the beach but don't expect to get Granny to walk it. It is not designed for one intolerant of rough trails. The beach is fantastic, however, since it is a large natural gravel bar that dives quickly into the green waters making it a favorite spot for many fisherman since it is easy to cast a line from shore.

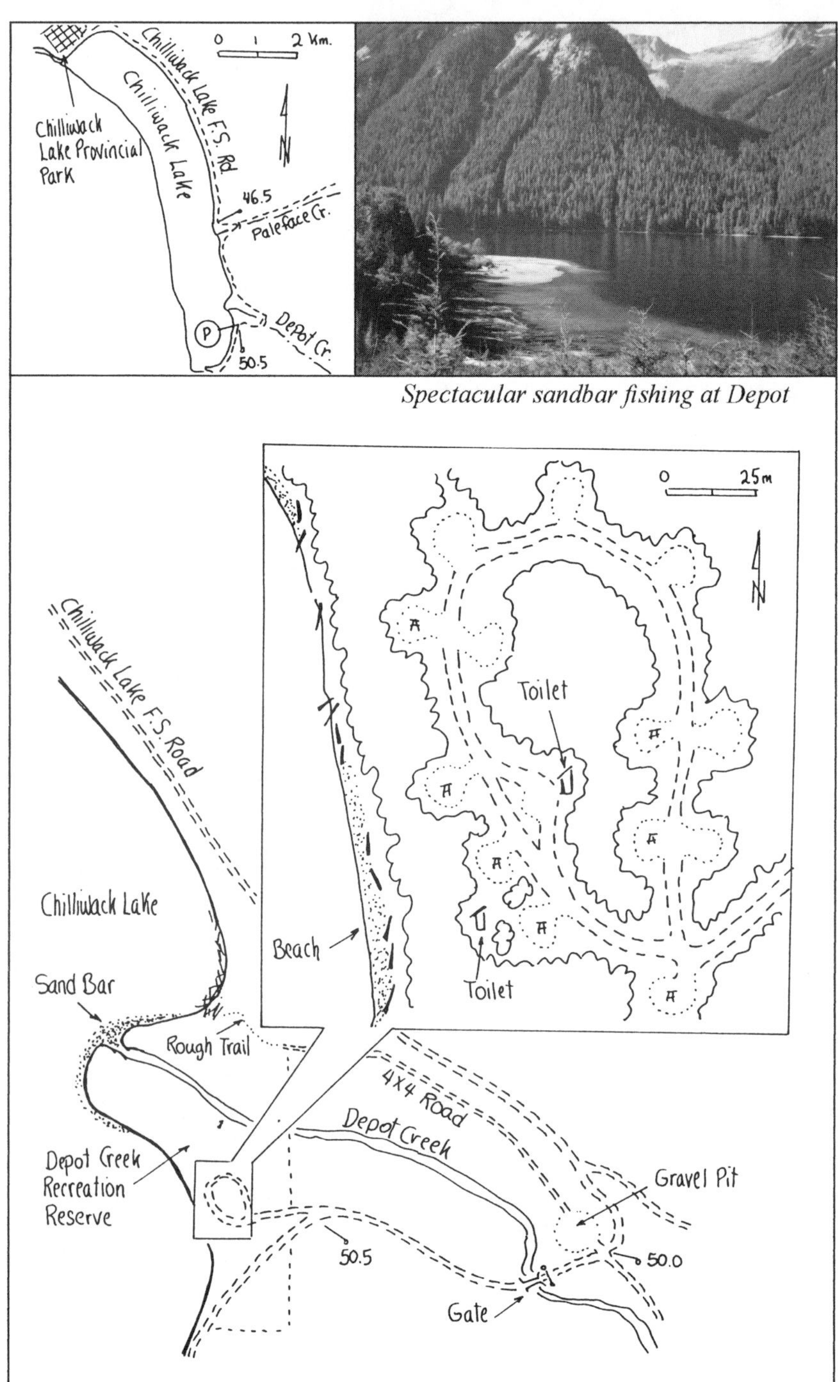

Spectacular sandbar fishing at Depot

SAPPERS PARK 36

☑ BEACH	☑ TENT CAMPING
☑ CANOEING	☑ SWIMMING
☑ FISHING	☑ VIEWING
☑ HIKING	☑ SMALL SITE

There are not too many fresh water lakes in the valley that offer a sandy beach, especially one that includes an impressive expanse of white sand. There is one place at the south end of Chilliwack Lake that fits the bill... cool water and miniature waves rolling in over a distance of several hundred meters. In mid summer, because of the expanse and shallowness of the water the sun will warm the beach water up to 5 degrees more than the lake water. At this end the Upper Chilliwack River surges out into the lake all winter pushing vast amounts of sand into the deep waters making the whole end a massive beach. In summer the river settles down to a slow moving flow. Then, as the lake waters recede, they expose a magnificent playground called Sappers Park.

The south end of Chilliwack Lake

FINDING the SITE From the Vedder Crossing, drive south along Vedder Road to take the Chilliwack Lake Road east. From this intersection you will clock 39.4 kilometers before you change to the Chilliwack Lake forest service road and pass the Chilliwack Lake Provincial Park. This road parallels the east shore of the lake all the way to the end, deteriorating gradually at the end but you can still use your car without grief, all the way to the end parking area. Note the Paleface Creek boat launch at 46.5 kilometers. This is the closest place where a trailered boat can be launched. You will pass the Paleface campsite at 46.9 kilometers and at 50.0 kilometers you will pass the open gravel areas before crossing Depot Creek. If the gate is closed, you may need to park and walk the last 2 kilometers to Sappers. If the gate is open, at the 50.5 kilometer mark, just over the bridge on the right there is a short road that drops to the beach area of the Depot Creek recreation site. Sappers Park is eventually reached at a distance of 52 kilometers. The road is blocked about 300 meters before Sappers Park so you will need to park on the wide shoulder and walk in.

SITE DESCRIPTION This is the farthest southern extent of Chilliwack-Lake. The Chilliwack River, which enters the lake at this point has pushed an enormous amount of sand and silt into the lake forming a large crescent shaped bay. As a result, the beach area is quite extensive, with the lakeshore sloping gently into the water over a distance of several hundred meters. Just back from the beach in the wooded area there are several camping pads but these are far and few between. There is a central biffy and some picnic tables.

SPECIAL FEATURES and ATTRACTIONS

Ecological Reserve and Upper Chilliwack River Trail The trailhead is opposite the beach area marked on the main road. From the trailhead at Sappers Park the trail curls around avoiding the large bend in the Chilliwack River. Within minutes the trail leads into the dark shade of the first growth giants, deep into the Ecological Reserve. From here on to the US border you alternate between the refreshing scenes along the Chilliwack River as it meanders towards the lake and the awesome cedars and firs that have stood there for centuries. The trail is flat rising only slightly following the rise in the river. As you marvel at these giants you will also have to stop and ponder at the endless shades of green created as the sun beams through the lofty canopy above. Most of the trail is like this providing an incredible living spectrum of delicate things in an ecosystem that has been this way, in balance, for a long time.

The US border is at 2.7 kilometers. Normally it should only take an hour but it is really hard to just walk through this forest without stopping and really inspecting this unique ecosystem, so allow two hours. You will have a few opportunities to sit beside the rushing river for a refreshing picnic, as have others, but there are no formal spots to do so. You will eventually hit the wide swath of cleared land marking our neighbor's land and the US border at the 49th parallel.

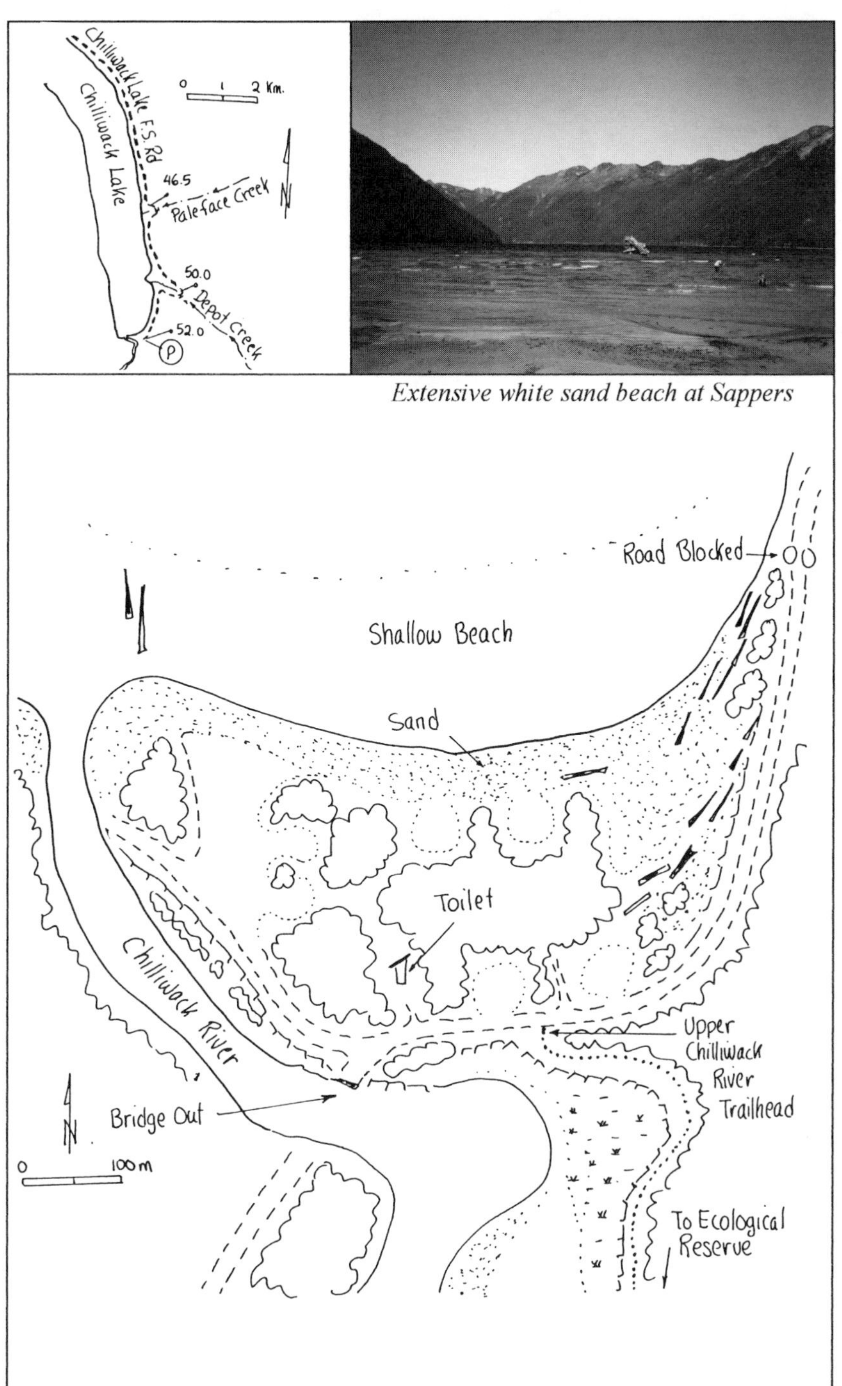

Extensive white sand beach at Sappers

EATON CREEK 37

☑ FISHING
☑ HIKING
☑ TENT CAMPING
☑ SMALL SITE

Not a particularly well endowed site, this place takes on much more significance when it is considered in conjunction with the Eaton Lake Trail. In this valley the Silverhope-Skagit river systems form an impressive drainage system through a unique mountainous area. This particular site gives one the opportunity to merge into this natural system and appreciate its rugged beauty. Not much more than a small picnic area and three camping pads, the Eaton Creek site serves as the trailhead for the impressive 6.5 kilometer trek into the rugged isolated valley at the head of Eaton Creek. Small and simple yet pleasant, this site is carefully positioned on a small wooded bench close to the main Silver-Skagit road, nicely hidden from view.

The tiny open area of the Eaton Creek site

FINDING the SITE The Silver Skagit Road is the main access route leading to the site. This particular road can take you 60 kilometers through the incredible Skagit Valley right to the US border. From Highway 1 just west of Hope take Exit 168 to Silver Creek, a little community along the old Flood Hope Road just on the outskirts of Hope. After taking this exit from the west, a short .3 kilometers along the Flood Hope Road takes you to Silver Skagit Road which turns north just before the bridge over Silverhope Creek. This is where you would zero your odometer. The road starts out paved but changes to a good gravel surface suitable for a car after a few kilometers. The road parallels Silverhope Creek up past the first branch at 6.1 kilometers. Remember this point if you want to visit the Silver Lake Provincial Park should the BCFS site be full. Continue on Silver Skagit Road past Silver Lake all the way to 16.4 kilometers where you will see a spur road climbing up the hill on the left. You should also see the familiar BCFS marker sign. The road is only a few hundred meters long stopping abruptly at the recreation site (and the local Eaton Lake trailhead to Eaton Lake). If you are driving a Corvette, you may want to leave it at the bottom.

SITE DESCRIPTION Right at the end of the short inclined road and the start of the trail, you will find some picnic tables, a biffy and a few grassy places to park. Don't get too excited about bringing in any larger recreation vehicles since open space, or turnaround area, is scarce. The area is small, sloping gradually toward the main road, opened up only in three places. Two sites provide a flat grassy area, each with a fire ring and a picnic table. The third higher up pad unfortunately serves as a parking lot. There is a biffy hidden in the trees across the road from the pads.

SPECIAL FEATURES and ATTRACTIONS The main attraction here is not the site but the Eaton Lake Trail. From the site you can take a 10 minute hike up the trail to reach Eaton Creek. This creek literally surges through a steep gorge. Even though it is not a large creek, it is cluttered with huge boulders, logs and stumps that it has torn out as it thunders and crashes furiously down the hill. It is well worth a short trip into this cool gorge. After this the trail steepens considerably, changing to a footpath and diverges from the creek. It intersects the creek again at the bridge, another 15 minutes farther.

Another attraction is the Skagit Valley and the Skagit River. This is a vast recreational playground at the southern end of the Silver Skagit Road, described under the Silverhope Site. Traveling back towards Hope, however, it is worth mentioning Silver Lake.

Silver Lake in the Silver Lake Provincial Park. It was just six short kilometers from the community of Silver Creek along the Silver Skagit Road, or a wee bit over 10 kilometers back from the Eaton Creek turnoff. Silver Lake, at 350 meters above sea level, is just over a kilometer in length, 40 hectares in size, offering a good-sized recreation area that has been recently upgraded to provide a good place for the whole family to enjoy, particularly if the Eaton site is full.

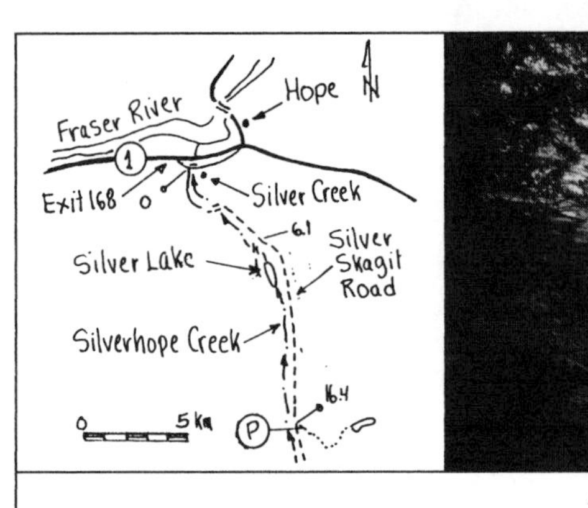

Parking space is limited

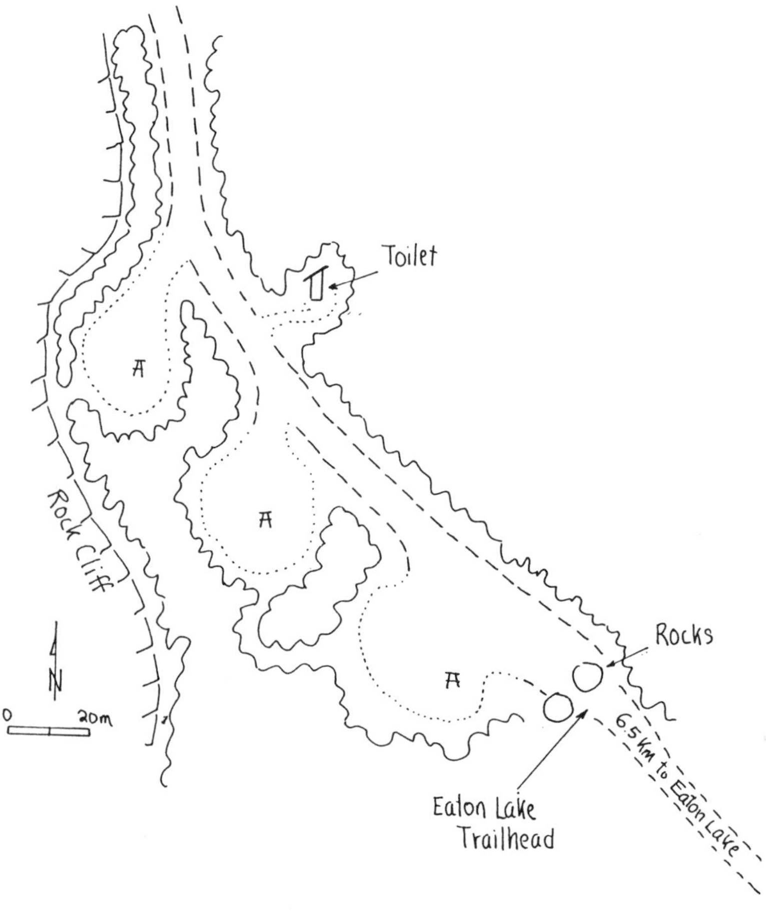

The facilities at the lake are classified as primitive, but obviously in the improvement stages. For a provincial park this is particularly unique but the campsites are well kept and very well positioned, providing a good variety of natural settings. The main sites are stretched out at the northwest side of the lake with several choice locations near the shore. The pit biffies are nicely centered and there is a water tap on the main road near site 22. At sites 28 and 29 it is possible to launch a cartop boat since they border a small gravel beach. There are several other nice campsites along a narrow bench that parallels the lake. The sites are semicircular open areas set in the trees, nestled against the rock bluff bordering the lakeshore, some having a small gravel beach where a boat/small trailer can be launched.

If you prefer a canoe or small boat this is a most incredible place to explore and fish. In the summer evenings the lake is typically dead still, making the water look like glass. You almost feel embarrassed to disturb it. Boat access is very good around much of the shoreline, further enticing you to get out there.

Silver Lake, like many other lakes in the region, contains a wide variety of game fish, including rainbow, kokanee, dolly varden and even Steelhead. They are typically small (around 20 to 25 centimeters). The lake is relatively shallow, reaching only 12 meters mid-lake. Much of the shoreline is shallow except the western campsite area where it drops fast to six meters. For the fly fisherman, the creek exit lagoon offers an incredible, inviting place to flick a fly. If you prefer to fish from shore there is a fast drop-off to ten meters right beside the road opposite the campsite. There is a sand bar at the south end of the lake where the creek enters.

SILVERHOPE 38

☑ TRAIL BIKING ☑ TENT CAMPING
☑ RECREATION VEHICLES ☑ SMALL SITE

This site used to be in the BCFS inventory but it is now closed. It does, despite the closure, still serve as a popular camping area for many who fail to find a spot at Silver Lake, or the Eaton Creek site. Since the next places to formally camp are many kilometers south at Silvertip and Ross Lake, this area serves quite a few "overflow" people. Sitting between the road and peaceful Siverhope Creek the site itself is not much more than a gravel bank where you can park, listen to the rush of the creek and roast a weenie. But... the *rest* of the area has much, much more. For this reason, rather than end the book on a small lonely and featureless site, I decided to describe the rest of the Skagit Valley.

Near the cool waters of Silverhope Creek

FINDING the SITE The access to the site is via the Silver Skagit Road from Silver Creek. You will have set your odometer to zero at this point at the start of the road by the bridge. The road will take you past the Silver Lake branch at 6.1 kilometers after which you will follow Silver Lake's shoreline. You will continue into the valley paralleling the beautiful rolling Silverhope Creek.

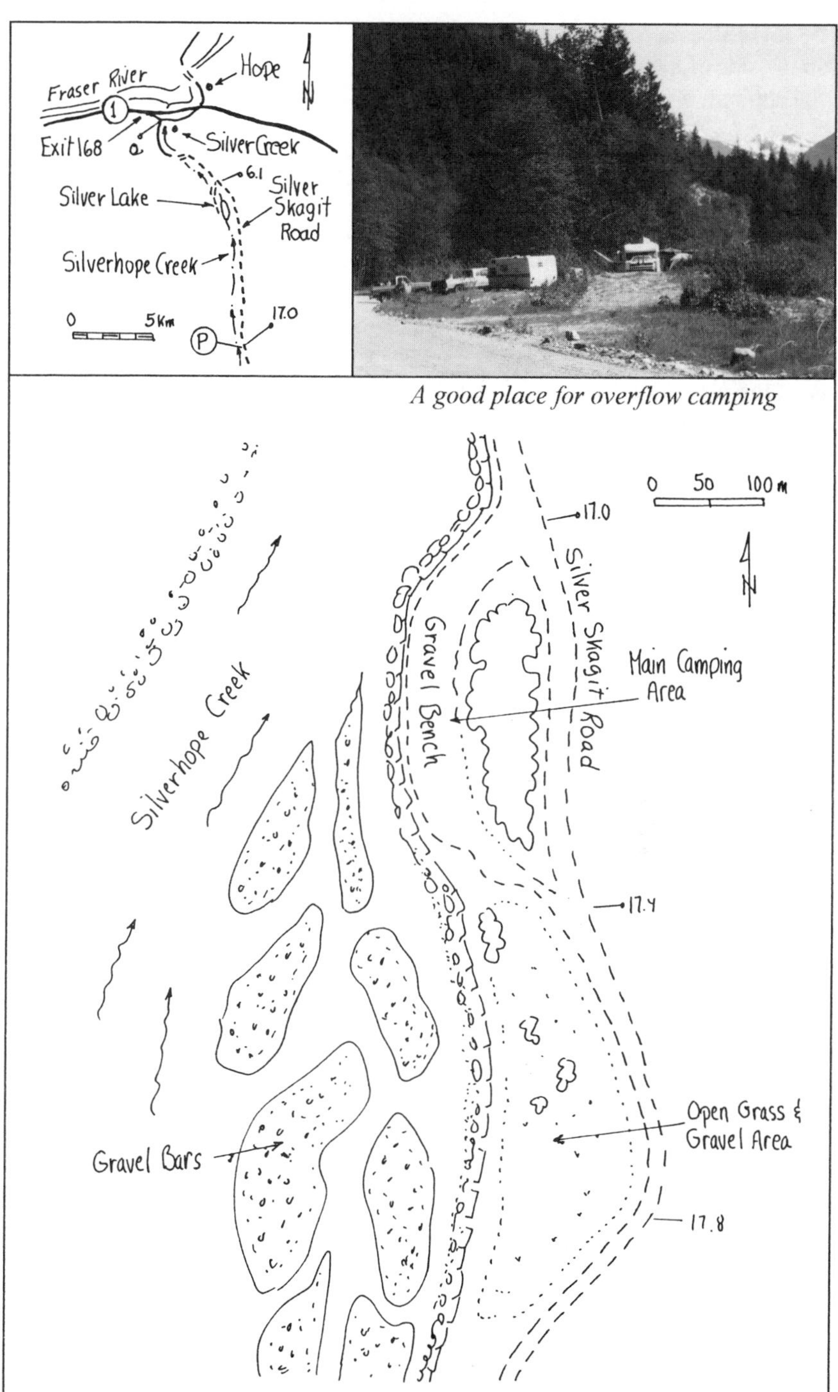

A good place for overflow camping

At 16.4 kilometers, you will note a Forest Service sign marking the short road up the side of the hill to the left at Eaton Creek. At 17 kilometers on your right, you can pull off onto a crescent-shaped gravel bank overlooking the creek.

SITE DESCRIPTION Not designed for the picky picnicker, the site is set along the Silverhope Creek at a location where the water has pushed and churned a mass of gravel. The main creek channel arcs around in wide swing for about a kilometer forming wide open gravel bars in the creek. Between these and the main road, an elevated gravel bench has formed providing the main camping area. The old site sits at the north end of the bench. There are no facilities here. A small grove of trees between the road and the camping bench is all the protection you can find here. Most of the bench is open and grassed to the south of the site, making it possible to camp anywhere along the kilometer stretch.

Eaton Lake Trail Your elevation will be about 440 meters at the start between the boulders at the Eaton Creek recreation site trailhead. The first 15 minutes is a pleasant walk through the timbers gaining elevation gradually on an old road. You soon come to the raging Eaton Creek as it roars down the gorge. The trail changes to a footpath switching back and forth, rising above the creek then crossing it via the bridge, gaining another 150 meters vertically. This is still less than a kilometer from the trailhead. From here you head away from the creek, eventually cutting back to it and the rest stop at 2.8 kilometers, elevation of 900 meters. From here, the ascent continues mercilessly until you reach an elevation of 1200 meters, at a distance of 5 kilometers. The last 1.5 kilometer flattens a bit, taking you to the west end of the lake at 1318 meters, a total of 6.5 kilometers from the trailhead. The elevation gain is from 440 meters to 1318 meters, a significant vertical change of 878 meters but you will be rewarded by scenes you will remember for a long time.

Eaton Lake This isolated lake is also called *Crescent Lake* sitting at an impressive elevation of 1318 meters, contains over 44 hectares of water trapped in a narrow crescent-like canyon. Guarded by Eaton Peak to the south, this higher-elevation "talus pocket lake" is dominantly broken rock that has fallen to line the lakeshore. Typically craggy bluffs surround these lakes, making them look like trapped pockets of water. Sub-alpine terrain is common to these valley pockets, always exposed to the harsh elements of 9 month winters. The lake is also reported to have 30 to 35-centimeter rainbow and cutthroat. These are relatively small but the cool water may have something to say about growth and survival rates. The lake is not stocked. Much of lakeshore has tough access with a log jammed outlet, wooded tangles and rock talus strewn into the lake from the cliffs. At the lake you will find few conveniences except for open pads used by others to pitch camp. There are no formal facilities here but they are really not required.

Skagit Valley Provincial Recreation Area This vast area covers about 32,000 hectares of wilderness prolific in raging streams, meandering rivers, massive stands of forest and impressive mountain peaks reaching 2200 meters. Straddling the southern part of the Silver Skagit road, the park starts at 35 kilometers from Highway 1 then extends all the way to the US border and Ross Lake another 26 kilometers south. Within this area there are endless natural attractions and many formal facilities that facilitate a wide range of recreational activities. Camping, hiking, nature observation, canoeing, swimming, boating, fishing, hunting, snowshoeing and ski touring are but a few. Within the main park for example you will find a 40 unit campground, located at the Silvertip. The Centennial Trail continues from the Chilliwack Valley across Custer Divide down Hicks Creek to the Silver Skagit Road and down to the Skagit River at a place called 26 mile Bridge. Here it joins the Skagit River Trail taking you 10 kilometers along the river all the way to Sumallo Grove on the Hope Princeton Highway and into the north section of the Cascade Recreation Area as well as the north west part of Manning Park. The Centennial Trail continues southeast along the Skagit River, then cuts east just before the Chittenden Bridge to intersect the massive network of trails in the south part of Manning Park. All together, this is a very extensive trail system.

Silverhope Creek and Skagit River Silverhope Creek, which passes through Silver Lake at the north part of the valley, tumbles over large boulders, forming a series of incredible pools along most of the road, easily accessed for much of its length, offering some fantastic fishing holes. The lake and creek combine to create a rather special recreation area. Silverhope Creek is large, connecting with the Fraser River so fish can swim freely in both stream and lake. Both are excellent spawning and feeding habitats. In fact the fishing is so fine it is illegal to keep fish under 20 centimeters and only single barbless hooks are allowed. The area is strictly protected from overzealous anglers so the regulations can change quickly... best to check these first.

The Skagit River is a whole different story. The area is famous for its slow moving waters that provide one of the most famous canoe and fly fishing opportunities in North America. It is one of the finest canoeable rivers around. Attracting the experienced river canoeists from July to fall, the river has many log jams alternating with slower moving clear waters deep enough to make excellent canoeing. The official launch is at 26 Mile Bridge, just past the entrance to the Silvertip Campground. For the fishermen this river also provides a quality sport fishing opportunity unequaled in the valley, as it alternates from deep long pools to quick runs of semi-whitewater. Deep enough for waders, and wide enough for fly casting, the bonus is that the river attracts large Steelhead and trout.

Galene Lakes These sit in a very unique place for those willing to tackle the adventure. A chain of small lakes are set high on the inside of Custer Ridge on the Skagit Valley side. Situated in a unique valley that can have frost all year round, these lakes are different than all the rest in the valley. The main Galene Lake sits at *1873 meters* in elevation, almost at the top of the ridge, definitely in the ice fields surrounding the ridge. This lake is the *highest* in the valley. Wright Peak, just a few kilometers north, reaches 2067 meters. To reach this place you need to tackle one of the more difficult trails in the valley. The trail is 16 kilometers long, taking you through the most incredible scenery you will ever find. A word of caution: this trail is for *experts* only.

The trailhead is on the Silver Skagit Road. From Silver Creek, at 35 kilometers you will enter the Skagit Valley recreation area and the famous slow-moving Skagit River. At 57.1 kilometers you will see the Chittenden footbridge crossing the Skagit River. This is a rather special piece of work difficult to miss, serving as the trailhead to the endurance test. From the Chittenden bridge, it is 16 kilometers to Galene Lake. The elevation gain is from 500 meters at the bridge to 1873 meters at lakeside. The first five kilometers are fairly easy but when you reach Galene Creek the trail loops around and switchbacks steeply to the ridge. From the switchback at an elevation of 750 meters the next two kilometers will lift you to 900 meters and the next two kilometers will take you to 1370 meters. The final five kilometers will lift you 500 meters more to lakeside at 1873.

Facilities at the lake include an informal BCFS site carved into the landscape. This is reported to be primitive but adequate. If you do decide to take this one on, it is always a good idea to check with the Forest Service to see if there are any changes to trails or facilities. There is no doubt this trail is also a feature of the area lifting you almost 1400 meters over a distance of 16 kilometers. You will climb from the valley floor through lush forests, along steep ridges to a place close to the permanent ice and snow line—if you move at a good pace and are in *excellent* shape. It will take you at *least* five to six hours one way, so be prepared and plan to stay overnight. *And* be prepared for weather changes. Most mortals will need the whole day! Most importantly you need to be experienced. If not, head down to Ross Lake for a picnic instead. This trail will lead you into an area that will give you the *true* definition of *remoteness*. The summer is short and the terrain is rugged. The weather can be unforgiving, unpredictable and brutal. I don't even think a cellular will work here. If you consider this trip let someone know, pick July and August for the trip, take a survival course and pack food for several days. Reports indicate 30 to 35-centimeter rainbow and cutthroat are in the lake, so at least you may not have to haul breakfast with you! It is hard to believe that this lake does not freeze solid every year.

Ross Lake is massive with only the northern tip of it in Canada. The lake was originally created by building the dam on the Skagit River in Washington. Over 35 kilometers long, this body of water is part of the Ross Lake National Recreation Area. Created by the hydroelectric dam, the lake barely pokes into the Canadian side after extending through the remote wilderness of the North Cascades National Park. There is a little place called Hozomeen at the very tip, marked by an old rusty gate across the gravel road at the border. The only way in is from the Canadian side and there is no access from the US to the south. On the US side there is a two-kilometer strip of road along the northeast side of the lake offering you a little taste of the US camping facilities. Needless to say, customs is not a serious matter here since there is nowhere to go. In fact, the customs official is more of a park ranger than anything else, a friendly man offering brochures and information on the park.

The lake itself is unusual at this end since it has flooded a vast marsh grass area. There are some excellent recreational facilities, particularly camping, on this end.

Access the lake and park is via Silver Skagit Road from Silver Creek. The trip is 58.7 kilometers to the Ross Lake Campground. The boat launch is .8 kilometers farther and the US border is just beyond that, down the left branch.

Facilities at the lake include a long list of conveniences. It is a *complete* recreational facility with 88 sites distributed along a long, thin section of the northeast tip of the lake. Most of the sites are set nicely in the woods offering nice shady cover, fire rings and a few picnic tables. Throughout the area you will find pit toilets, firewood and water taps and there is a large picnic area to the south near the cove. In the same area you will find a good gravel boat launch and swimming area. There is a group campsite and there are various hiking trails in the area.

If, for some reason, these facilities are full just drive down to the US side and you will find many nice sites along the lakeshore. In many respects these are better than those on the Canadian side. Since the road dead-ends a few kilometers after the border, there is really a bit of an imaginary border here. Just stop at the gate and say hello.

There are various trails on the US side with an ecological reserve as well. The Hozomeen Trail is the most popular, about five kilometers long accessed from the US side near the end of the road, taking you up to Hozomeen Lake. In fact this trail connects with Willow Lake, Lightening Creek and the East Bank Trail, taking you all the way down to the south dam 35 kilometers away. It then connects with other North Cascades Trails.

INDEX TABLE

RECREATION SITE CHARACTERISTICS SUMMARY

Site number → Site situated on → Vehicle access by → Type of boat or launch → Beach activities

Site Name	Site number	Site situated on	Vehicle access by	Type of boat or launch	Beach activities	Page
Allison Pool	24	Riverside	Car	None	None	115
Bear Creek	21	Lakeshore	Car	Gravel beach	Swim	105
Camp Foley	27	Riverside	Car	Kayak	None	125
Cascade Peninsula	20	Lakeside	Boat	Boat only	Swim	101
Chehalis Lake North	8	Lakeside	Car	Gravel beach	Swim	51
Chehalis River	9	Riverside	Car	None	None	55
Chehalis Lake South	6	Lakeside	Truck	Concrete pads	Swim	43
Chipmunk Peninsula	28	Riverside	Car	Kayak	None	128
Cogburn Beach	22	Lakeside	Car	Gravel beach	Swim	108
Cypress Point	2	Lakeside	Truck	Gravel bar	None	28
Depot Creek	35	Lakeside	Car	Sand beach	Swim	154
Eagles Roost	30	Riverside	Car	Kayak	None	134
Eaton Creek	37	Forest	Car	None	None	160
Foley Lake	31	Lakeside	Car	Sand beach	None	137
Francis Lake	13	Lakeside	Truck	Gravel launch	None	73
Grace Lake	11	Lakeside	Car	Muddy shore	None	65
Hale Creek	15	Lakeside	4X4	Sand beach	Swim	81
Kenyon Lake	4	Lakeside	Truck	Muddy shore	None	36
Long Island Bay	17	Lake	Boat	Boat only	Swim	89
Paleface Creek	34	Creekside	Car	Concrete pads	Swim	150
Pierce Creek	26	Forest	Car	None	None	121
Post Creek	33	Creekside	Car	None	None	145
Rainbow Falls	19	Lakeside	Boat	Boat only	Swim	97
Rapids	29	Riverside	Car	Kayak	None	131
Riverside	32	Riverside	Car	None	None	141
Salsbury Lake	3	Lakeside	Car	Gravel path	None	32
Sappers Park	36	Lakeside	Car	Sand beach	Swim	157
Siverhope	38	Riverside	Car	None	None	164
Skwellepil Creek	7	Lakeside	Truck	Gravel beach	Swim	47
Sunrise Lake	16	Lakeside	4X4	Muddy shore	None	85
Tamihi Creek	23	Riverside	Car	Kayak	None	111
Thurston Meadows	25	Riverside	Car	None	None	118
Twenty Mile Creek	18	Lakeside	Car	Gravel beach	Swim	93
Twin Bridges	5	Creekside	Car	None	None	40
Weaver Creek	10	Lakeside	Truck	Gravel launch	None	60
Widgeon Lake	1	Creekside	Boat	Sand beach	Swim	22
Wolf Lake	12	Lakeside	Truck	Muddy shore	None	69
Wood Lake	14	Lakeside	Car	Gravel beach	None	77

Site Characteristics are also summarized in alphabetical order to provide you with the ability to scan the main recreational features at the site or close to the site. You will find all the key information but these are only general descriptions. Please refer to the actual write-up for details.

INDEX TABLE

RECREATION SITE FACILITIES AND ACTIVITIES SUMMARY

Site Name	Board sailing	Boating	Canoeing	Tenting	Recreation vehicles	Hiking	Fishing	Viewing	Beach activities	Swimming	Trail biking	Kayaking	Page
Allison Pool				✓	✓		✓						115
Bear Creek			✓	✓			✓			✓			105
Camp Foley				✓	✓							✓	125
Cascade Peninsula		✓	✓	✓			✓		✓	✓			101
Chehalis Lake North		✓	✓	✓	✓	✓	✓		✓	✓	✓		51
Chehalis River				✓	✓	✓	✓	✓					55
Chehalis Lake South		✓	✓	✓	✓		✓			✓	✓		43
Chipmunk Peninsula				✓	✓						✓	✓	128
Cogburn Beach			✓	✓	✓				✓	✓			108
Cypress Point		✓	✓	✓	✓	✓	✓				✓		28
Depot Creek			✓	✓	✓		✓		✓	✓			154
Eagles Roost				✓	✓							✓	134
Eaton Creek				✓	✓	✓							160
Foley Lake			✓	✓	✓	✓	✓				✓		137
Francis Lake			✓	✓			✓						73
Grace Lake			✓	✓	✓		✓						65
Hale Creek		✓	✓	✓			✓			✓			81
Kenyon Lake			✓	✓			✓				✓		36
Long Island Bay		✓	✓	✓					✓	✓			89
Paleface Creek		✓	✓	✓	✓		✓		✓	✓	✓		150
Pierce Creek				✓		✓							121
Post Creek				✓	✓	✓							145
Rainbow Falls		✓	✓	✓			✓			✓			97
Rapids				✓	✓							✓	131
Riverside				✓		✓					✓		141
Salsbury Lake		✓	✓	✓	✓		✓				✓		32
Sappers Park				✓		✓		✓	✓	✓			157
Silverhope				✓	✓	✓							164
Skwellepil Creek		✓	✓	✓		✓	✓			✓	✓		47
Sunrise Lake			✓	✓			✓						85
Tamihi Creek				✓	✓		✓				✓	✓	111
Thurston Meadows				✓	✓		✓						118
Twenty Mile Creek	✓	✓	✓	✓	✓				✓	✓	✓		93
Twin Bridges				✓	✓						✓		40
Weaver Creek		✓	✓	✓	✓	✓	✓						60
Widgeon Lake		✓	✓	✓		✓		✓		✓			22
Wolf Lake			✓	✓	✓		✓						69
Wood Lake			✓	✓	✓		✓						77

Site Facilities and Activities Summary provides you with a quick look at the main recreational conveniences and the type of activities suited to the area. For detailed descriptions please refer to the write-up in the main text.

Index

Contact Numbers

The following list is provided for those who may need to find more information on the lakes, parks, roads and services in the Lower Fraser Valley. Please keep in mind that *numbers may change*.

CANADIAN FOREST PRODUCTS (Harrison Mills) **796-2757**
This number is useful to determine the logging road states, closures, times open, and to get general information on access in the Harrison Region.

BC FOREST SERVICE
Rosedale Office (direct line from Vancouver) **685-5972**
Rosedale Office (local line) **794-2100**
For information on the status or state of BCFS sites and trails, call this number.

HUNTING and FISHING
Maple Ridge Office **465-4011**
Chilliwack Office **795-8422**
These are conservation offices that will give you up to date information on fishing (excluding salmon) or hunting regulations.

MAPS
Geological Survey of Canada **666-0271**
Wide World of Books and Maps **687-3320**
These two numbers will get you up to date, good quality, topographic and road maps covering the area.

ROYAL CANADIAN MOUNTED POLICE
Maple Ridge and Pitt Meadows (Maple Ridge) **463-6251**
Hope and Skagit (Hope) **869-7750**
Mission to Lake Errock (Mission) **462-0673**
Agassiz and Harrison (Agassiz) **796-2211**
Chilliwack to Rosedale (Chilliwack) **792-4611**
You may need these numbers if you have troubles requiring police attention.

WEATHER FORECASTS (Environment Canada)
General Information and Administration **664-9032**
Greater Vancouver **664-9010**
Fraser Valley **664-9021**
These numbers are great for up to date recorded weather conditions and forecasts in the area.

More Outdoors Books by Ed Rychkun

TROUT FISHING
The Tactical Secrets of Lake Fishing
Ed Rychkun

Ed Rychkun, 120 pages
ISBN 0-88839-338-5
Reveals fish behavior, physiology and habits as they relate to successful fishing tactics, with "on the water examples".

Guide to Salmon Fishing
The Best Fishing Holes of Campbell River and Barkley Sound
Ed Rychkun
Mike Rychkun

Ed Rychkun and Mike Rychkun, 96 pages
ISBN 0-88839-305-9
Detailed navigational charts with water depths, and fishing hole characteristics, detailing the most productive holes and fishing tactics.

195 LAKES of the Fraser Valley Volume I
West Vancouver to Stave Falls
Ed Rychkun

A recreational Guide to:
- Backroad Exploring
- Boating
- Camping
- Fishing
- Hiking
- Horesback Riding
- Picnicking

Ed Rychkun, 238 pages
ISBN 0-88839-339-3
A complete guide on how to find every lake in the valley, from Vancouver to Stave Falls, with all recreational facilities, features and attractions detailed, including water depth contours plus hundreds of detailed maps.

195 LAKES of the Fraser Valley Volume II
Dewdney to Hope
Ed Rychkun

A recreational Guide to:
- Backroad Exploring
- Boating
- Camping
- Fishing
- Hiking
- Horesback Riding
- Picnicking

Ed Rychkun, 272 pages
ISBN 0-88839-377-6
A complete guide on how to find every lake in the valley, from Dewdney to Hope, with all recreational facilities, features and attractions detailed, including water depth contours plus hundreds of detailed maps.

The

12 BASIC SKILLS

of FLY FISHING

Ted Peck &

Ed Rychkun

Ted Peck & Ed Rychkun, 40 pages

ISBN 0-88839-392-X

This concise booklet tells the secrets of the art... directly from the fly fishing master Ted Peck. All Ted's decades of experience come together in this special book to take the mystery and complications out of fly fishing.

The master's secrets are illustrated by Ed Rychkun, taken directly from Ted's popular night school sessions.

This book is guaranteed to simplify the art and let you sweep that fly line in an elegant cast within a few days.

Don't miss the companion book to the BC Forest Camping

Ed Rychkun, 112 pages

ISBN 0-9681357-0-6

Wilderness Trails reveals all those special hiking trails created and maintained by the B.C. Forest Service. Twenty-one unique trails are covered in explicit detail showing scaled contour maps and elevation profiles. Over 40 pictures will reveal the key features and attractions along the trails. These exceptional trails cover over 100 kilometers of ecologically conscious trails, created to ensure minimal disturbance to the natural wilderness yet allow you to enjoy some unbelievable, unique scenery. Many trails are challenging so a special section on trail technology is included.

- detailed trailhead location maps
- mileage markers and landmarks
- access requirements
- critical statistics summary
- individual endurance calculations
- detailed elevations contours
- trail profiles with key features
- quick look-up/summary tables
- local features and attractions
- relevant facilities and sights